Aesthetic Protest Cultures:
After the Avant-Garde

Edited by Mikkel Bolt Rasmussen

<.:.Min0r.:.>
.c0mp0siti0ns.

Aesthetic Protest Cultures: After the Avant-Garde
Edited by Mikkel Bolt Rasmussen

ISBN 978-1-57027-452-7

Cover design by Haduhi Szukis
Interior design by Casandra Johns

Released by Minor Compositions 2024
Colchester / New York / Port Watson

Minor Compositions is a series of interventions & provocations drawing from autonomous politics, avant-garde aesthetics, and the revolutions of everyday life.

Minor Compositions is an imprint of Autonomedia
www.minorcompositions.info | minorcompositions@gmail.com

Distributed by Autonomedia
PO Box 568 Williamsburgh Station
Brooklyn, NY 11211

www.autonomedia.org
info@autonomedia.org

For Marina

Contents

No Wising Up and No Settling Down: Introductory Notes on the Question of the Avant-Garde

Mikkel Bolt Rasmussen

"The dead speak and people riot as a kind of revolutionary mourning practice, and this happens unpredictably."

– Hannah Black[1]

Where to begin? The war in Ukraine has raged for more than 450 days now. The Russian invasion of Ukraine came as a surprise to most people, and even though there is no doubt that Putin is engaged in an imperialist invasion of a former colony, it is not difficult to see how the war has quickly become an inter-imperialist conflict, where Washington is using not only NATO members like Poland and the UK, but also Zelensky against Russia, and all the while preparing for a large-scale conflict with China.[2] Geopolitical rivalries are on the rise, a Chinese invasion of Taiwan is a possibility, and avoiding the mirroring effects of national chauvinist war myths has proved exceedingly difficult. Given our current situation, it seems important to

---

1   Hannah Black in interview with Larne Abse Gogarty: "Burning Issues," *Art Monthly*, no. 441, 2020, 4.

2   For a good analysis of the war, see the different articles by Andrew, the most recent one being: "Untimely Thoughts: Notes on Revolution and Ukraine," *Insurgent Notes*, no. 25, 2022, http://insurgentnotes.com/2022/12/untimely-thoughts-notes-on-revolution-and-ukraine/

zoom out and emphasise the context of the war: the extended world economic crisis since the last global revolt between 1968 and 1977: from the May '68 protests to the 77-movement in Italy. A lengthy list of economists and historians, Marxist and bourgeois, Michael Roberts, Karl Heinz Roth, Endnotes, Adam Tooze and many others have described capitalism's inability to solve the overaccumulation crisis confronting us since the early 1970s.[3] Economic development in the 1980s and 1990s took the form of credit and the search for cheaper workers. For more than three decades, debt and the relocation of production facilitated greater exploitation of wage labour and combined to conceal overproduction and falling investments. The 'globalisation' of the economy is now being replaced by geopolitical conflicts causing rapid rearmament, inflation, and higher prices for raw materials. The global market is undergoing radical reorganisation. Post-war consensus about political democracy has again given way to nationalist politicians who stress the need to protect 'their' working classes.

If the financial crisis, on the one hand, made visible the critical condition of *gesamt* capital, it also confirmed global neoliberalism's extended reach, with central banks flooding markets with money without any increase in investment, resulting in an escalation in both private and public debt. When the pandemic hit in 2020 – itself a product of the extraction of nature by the capitalist mode of production – governments worldwide had no other solution than to pump enormous sums of money into the global economy, although this has in no way led to higher investment. Without a rate of return, this will never happen, and excess capital will inevitably always find its way

---

3   Endnotes: "The Holding Pattern," *Endnotes*, no. 3, 2013, 12-54; Michael Roberts: *The Long Depression: Marxism and the Global Crisis of Capitalism* (Chicago: Haymarket, 2016); Karl Heinz Roth: *Die lange Depression* (Hamburg: VSA Verlag, 2014); Adam Tooze: *Shutdown: How COVID Shook the World's Economy* (New York: Viking, 2021).

into different forms of speculative investment, such as stocks or the property market. Consumer prices are on the way up, and Western democracies are tightening their already exclusionary policies. The UK intends to send refugees to Rwanda, the Greek coastguard has fired warning shots at migrants or has left them in the Mediterranean on boats with disabled motors, and in the US, Texas Republican Governor Greg Abbott has deployed more than 10,000 National Guards to the Mexican border.[4]

The situation does not look good. We have an enduring capitalist crisis, a pandemic, and ever-mounting geopolitical conflicts. Not to mention a climate crisis, which very much embodies capitalist modernity's potential to destroy both human and more-than-human life in its entirety.[5] The ruling political and economic order seems bereft of problem-solving solutions, not least to the ecological disasters, the mass extinction of animals and plants, global warming, rising sea levels, fires, pollution and poisoning, pandemics and climate chaos. The global South is being ravaged by all of these developments, and it is only a matter of time before everyone else is affected, too.

---

4   Diane Taylor: "Home Office in fresh row with UNHCR over Rwanda asylum policy," *Guardian*, 17 July 2022, https://www.theguardian.com/uk-news/2022/jul/17/home-office-in-fresh-row-with-unhcr-over-rwanda-asylum-policy; Julia Pascual & Marina Rafenberg: "Aux frontières grecques, les réfugiés continuent d'être refoulés," *Le Monde*, 17 April 2022, https://www.lemonde.fr/international/article/2022/04/17/aux-frontieres-grecques-les-refugies-continuent-d-etre-refoules_6122501_3210.html; Lomi Kriel & Perla Trevizo: "Gov. Greg Abbot brags about his border initiative: The evidence doesn't back him up," *The Texas Tribune*, 21 March 2022, https://www.texastribune.org/2022/03/21/operation-lone-star-lacks-clear-metrics-measure-accomplishments/

5   As geologists have convincingly argued, we have left the holocene, a 11,650 year long period with a relatively stable climate on Earth, cf. Jan Zalasiewicz, Colin N. Waters and Mark Williams (eds.), *The Anthropocene as a Geological Unit: A Guide to the Scientific Evidence and Current Debate* (Cambridge: Cambridge University Press, 2019).

It is no secret that capitalism is barbaric, but it seems as if the overall systemic destruction is growing in scale: Today, 50% of children in the world survive on less than five dollars a day, and 20% of all children do not go to school. Every day, more than 10,000 people die of poverty-related issues: that is, one human being every four seconds. At the same time, the ten wealthiest people in the world have amassed more than the 40% poorest, and the 20 richest people in the world emit 8,000 times more carbon than the poorest one billion.[6]

For a long period, beginning with the post-war economic boom, intense accumulation went hand in hand with mass consumption. In the following four decades, as the post-world war welfare state was slowly dismantled, the structural violence was less visible to the naked eye. At least in the West. If we zoom out, the period since the mid-1970s begins to take on the shape of a prolonged nightmare: military dictatorships in Latin America, the repression of radical elements during the Iranian Revolution, the return of fundamentalist Islamism, war and hunger in large parts of Africa, and social misery in Eastern Europe and the former Soviet Union after the fall of the Berlin Wall. China and South-East Asia were seen as positive stories, but even there, we find evidence that capital leads to just as much disaster and destruction as development.[7] From this perspective, what is taking place right now in the old centres of accumulation resembles normalisation. The six decades from 1948 to 2008 were the exception, not the rule. The horrors of capitalism are no longer disguised by debt and local consumption. Militarism, racism, sexism, and transphobia are now the order of the day.

---

6   Cf. Oxfam: "Inequality Kills," January 2022, https://oxfamilibrary.openrepository. com/bitstream/handle/10546/621341/bp-inequality-kills-170122-summ-en.pdf

7   Amadeo Bordiga: "Murder of the Dead" [1951], *The Science and Passion of Communism* (Leiden: Brill, 2020), 315-326.

However, there are also other things going on. Since 2010, millions of people have taken to the streets to reject this new order. Protests obviously took place between 1980 and 2010 (not least the demonstrations on Tiananmen Square in 1989, which deserve particular mention), but since 2010 we have witnessed a veritable explosion in the number and scale of protests, riots, strikes and revolts around the globe. As Alain Bertho and Joshua Clover, among others, have argued, we are living in "an era of uprisings."[8] The economic crisis and the heavy-handed management of its effects have bought people into the streets. If we cannot say the present situation is producing revolutionaries, as Debord and the Situationists believed after May '68, it at least appears to produce discontented subjects who refuse to accept economic misery and state control as the norm.[9] The years 2011 and 2019 marked high points in a discontinuous wave of protest that moved staccato-like across the globe, from the Arab Spring revolts in Tunisia, Egypt, Bahrain, Yemen, and Syria, to the central square occupations movements in Southern Europe, Turkey, Israel and the US, and onwards to students protests in Chile and Canada, Maidan in Ukraine in 2013–2014, the 'democracy' protests in Hong Kong, the roundabout occupations in France, protests against racist police violence in the US, and the Sudan commune. Not even the pandemic could halt the demonstrations. The George Floyd protests in the summer of 2020 were the largest of their kind in American history, more all-encompassing than the mid-1960s race riots: a police station was burned down, and whole neighbourhoods were liberated from police control. In 2020, India was the scene of the largest general strike in history, with more than 250 million people stopping work

---

8   Alain Bertho: *Le temps des émeutes* (Paris: Bayard, 2009); Joshua Clover: *Riot. Strike. Riot: The New Era of Uprisings* (London & New York: Verso, 2016).

9   Situationist International: "The Beginning of an Era" [1969], *Bureau of Public Secrets*, http://www.bopsecrets.org/SI/12.era1.htm

in protest against deteriorating working conditions and lower prices for agricultural products. Since then, we have had protesters storming the halls of power in Sri Lanka, an insurrection in Kazakhstan where protesters set light to government buildings and a feminist uprising in Iran, described by Asef Bayat as a revolution.[10] In China, the number of 'events' is also on the rise – 'events' being the authorities' designation of protests and strikes – with riots at Foxconn and large-scale demonstrations against draconian lockdown measures during the pandemic.

Many protests have been vigorously suppressed, including in countries like the US and France, where the police have responded with full force. The apocalyptic violence of the civil war in Syria stands as a warning to protesters everywhere. No effort is spared to prevent protests from developing into alternatives. Reactionary politicians such as Trump, Bolsonaro, and Meloni embrace discontent as a vehicle for fascist programmes that short-circuit the protests' criticisms, channelling them into xenophobia and campaigns against socially constructed 'others.' Right now, it seems that it is mainly the late fascists who are capable of mediating popular protest.[11] The older, traditional political parties and the trade unions appear unable to tackle the task at hand. The distance between institutional order and its extraneous reality comes across as a gaping chasm, and the resulting protests will no doubt continue apace.

---

10   Interview with Asef Bayat, originally published in Farsi by the Iranian daily *Etemad*, but quickly removed from the homepage: "A New Iran Has Been Born – A Global Iran," *New Lines Magazine*, 26 October 2022, https://newlinesmag.com/argument/a-new-iran-has-been-born-a-global-iran/

11   Cf. Mikkel Bolt Rasmussen: *Late Capitalist Fascism* (Cambridge: Polity, 2022).

Art and Revolution

Examining artistic practices in a situation where the violence of capital is rising, where more and more people are taking to the streets while sophisticated contemporary art is busy organising fashion shows for Dior, may seem strange, but modern art was from the get-go one of the few places where it was conceivable and possible – not that it was easy – to imagine the world differently.[12] This is why T.J. Clark, in *Farewell to An Idea,* details modern art and its relation to the workers' movement and socialism, writing that modern art was an attempt to give capitalist modernity a different shape beyond wage labour and the nation state.[13] Not that they were ever identical, modern art and socialism, but they were closely related. Art as revolutionary politics, and politics as an attempt to supersede capitalism. There was no agreement as to the form this supersession might take: The many debates about the politics of transition were a testament to that, but it was genuinely believed that it was possible not only to challenge the ruling order, but actually to transition out of it. This is evidently no longer the case.

The crisis appears different to us now than it did for the Surrealists in the inter-war period or the Situationists in the economic boom of the post-war era. They, too, were confronted with an accelerating political-economic dynamic that made it increasingly difficult to orient oneself and come to grips with

---

12   It is obviously Claire Fontaine's collaboration with Dior that I am referring to here. Claire Fontaine created the scenography for the 2020 Dior defile in Paris, including 15 neon signs with short sentences like: "Patriarchy = CO2" and "Women's Love is Unpaid Labor." For an analysis, see Mikkel Bolt Rasmussen and Dominique Routhier: "Farewell to (Bourgeois) Art Criticism," *Paletten,* no. 325, 2021, 60-70.

13   T.J. Clark: *Farewell to An Idea: Episodes from a History of Modernism* (New Haven: Yale University Press, 1999), 8-10.

the surrounding situation, possibilities and challenges. Particularly the Surrealists' arrival on the scene was notably belated: the proletarian offensive was already on the wane when the group was established in 1924. They were forced to position themselves vis-à-vis a rapidly degenerating Soviet state capitalist order that did – or did not – constitute an alternative to a crisis-ridden private capitalism lurching from one bizarre emergency solution to another, from Mussolini to Hitler in the space of a mere 15 years. It was no-less complicated for the Situationists: they bore witness to an intense expansion of the capacity to fetishise the political economy whereby capital gained access to control of the human imagination. Mass media, art, and politics fused together in the society of the spectacle. The Situationists described this development as the "colonisation of everyday life," comparable to the 'first' colonisation: the plundering, enslaving, and establishment of sea routes around the globe. The workers back at home were easier to control once given access to coffee, sugar, and opiates from the colonies. Nonetheless, the Surrealists and Situationists were confident that a new world was waiting within the decaying capitalist one they already inhabited. They shared this belief with the various socialist movements, be they Leninist or Social Democratic, Third-Worldist or Council Communist: they all saw the existing order from the perspective of transformational potential.

Anyone who has read a Situationists' journal or looked at a painting by Yves Tanguy or Leonora Carrington knows that the avant-gardes in no way subscribed to the established worker's movement's idea of progress, productivity and joy in hard labour. The avant-gardes had nothing but contempt for the various socialist notions of a self-righteous masculine work culture characterised by hard physical labour and asceticism. They tried to gesture towards and produce other forms of life, but they were engaged in the same project in some way or another nevertheless – a project to push modern capitalist civilisation in a different direction. In the case of the avant-gardes, this consisted of setting up an alternative community outside the framework of the nation and not mediated by money and commodities.

Some of the difficulties encountered by the avant-gardes centred on either the form of socialism or the Left's gradual acceptance of capital accumulation and the way the nation state is configured. The fact that the Left – the German Social Democrats being a case in point as early as 1914 – not only started to operate within the framework of the modern national democratic class society but stopped gesturing towards a world beyond the economy, wage labour and capital. As Walter Benjamin put it in 1921 in his text on violence, the established workers' movement had ceased to question the state form of power.[14] The brutal crackdown by the German Social Democrats on the German Revolution in 1919 confirmed this. With this in mind, we should qualify Clark's description by stating that modernism, and primarily avant-garde groups such as the Surrealists and the Situationists, were more closely aligned to a wild socialism that sought to create a life that consisted of more than wage labour, parliament and the family.[15] In other words, outside the established reformist section of the working-class movement.

We can perhaps put it like this: the avant-gardes were an integral part of a revolutionary tradition. This also explains why modernism was not a style but a programme. "Architecture

---

14   Walter Benjamin: "Critique of Violence" [1921], *Selected Writings. Volume I: 1913-1926* (Cambridge, MA: Harvard University Press, 1996), 246.

15   For a good description of the different currents of wild socialism, see Charles Reeve: *Le socialism sauvage. Essai sur l'auto-organisation et la démocratie directe dans les luttes de 1789 à nos jours* (Paris: L'échappée, 2018).

and revolution," as the Soviet Constructivists proclaimed.[16] It was about creating a different society.

In retrospect, the Soviet avant-garde exemplifies this approach more than any other group. Hundreds of artists dedicated themselves to a grandiose design project as part of which everything, all the objects and things we use in everyday life, had to be rethought and given a new form that corresponded to the new society that was being set up. A society characterised by autonomy and equality. A pair of trousers in the new communist society could not be the same as those in the capitalist US. The passive capitalist commodity had to be replaced by an active socialist object, as Boris Arvatov argued.[17] The avant-garde artists understood that it was necessary to communise society and that it was of the utmost importance to begin an immediate and all-pervasive transformation of society. The production of a new wo/man could not be postponed, and it was impossible to separate economic, political, and cultural struggles. The avant-garde understood the importance of everyday life: it had to be transformed, art and everyday life were to merge in a revolutionary process. The revolution was not just ownership of the means of production changing hands, i.e., workers' control; the revolution was a complete and immediate change in how people live. It was not to be: the

---

16   Contrary to Le Corbusier who concluded his manifesto for a new architecture by writing that a revolution could be prevented by the inventing of new architectural forms: "Society is filled with a violent desire for something which it may obtain or may not. Everything lies in that: everything depends on the effort made and the attention paid to these alarming symptoms. Architecture or Revolution. Revolution may be avoided." Le Corbusier: *Towards a New Architecture* [1923] (New York: Dover, 1986), 288-289.

17   For a great analysis of the notion of socialist objects and the communisation the Soviet avant-garde sought to realise before it was too late and the doctrine of Socialist Realism was introduced, see Christina Kiaer: *Imagine No Possessions: The Socialist Objects of Russian Constructivism* (Cambridge, MA & London: MIT Press, 2005).

Russian Revolution was quickly reduced to wielding political power over a society that had failed to transform as envisaged.

The avant-garde had a very particular understanding of revolution that developed during and immediately after the proletarian revolutions in the years from 1917 to 1921. Their revolution was not about power; it was about experimenting with new ways of living. Right here, right now. It was not enough just to seize power. It had to be totally dismantled – immediately. The Situationist critique of Lenin and the Bolsheviks encapsulated this point of view: they had taken power but clung on to it, forgot to change society, up to and including upholding capital as the primary means of distribution.[18] As Anatole Kopp has meticulously demonstrated in his books, Soviet revolutionary art and architecture were supposed to contribute to this transformation by producing forms that served as "social condensers," where the artwork was both an image of the coming life and a medium for the creation of that life.[19] In this way, the avant-garde was both an affirmation and an inversion of the modernist art ideology, according to which the artwork contains a potential and creates images of another world, because it does not obey externally set rules.

This is the avant-garde we need to keep in mind. The avant-garde as a process of revolutionary social transformation, not the avant-garde as the spearhead in a linear and progressive historical development. The avant-garde was the most

---

18   As Guy Debord put it in 1967: "The Bolshevik party justified itself in terms of the necessity of a State monopoly over the representation and defense of the power of the workers, and its success in this quest turned the party into what it truly was, namely the party of the owners of the proletariat, which essentially dislodged all earlier forms of ownership." Guy Debord: *The Society of the Spectacle* [1967] (New York: Zone, 1995), 70.

19   Anatole Kopp: *Changer la vie, changer la ville. De la vie nouvelle aux problèmes urbains U.R.S.S 1917-1932* (Paris: Union Générale d'Éditions, 1975), 42.

self-critical part of Euro-modernity when the work of art was a revolutionary experiment that intervened in both the base and superstructure with a view to producing an alternative community. A community beyond all the different bourgeois notions of nationality, property, family, and the individual. The avant-gardes participated in the formulation of an anti-national community that wreaked havoc in what Sylvia Wynter calls "techno-industrial Progress and national-racial Manifest Destiny."[20] The avant-garde did not make it that far, ending up stuck in the anti-national gesture. However, it provides a good starting point in the current climate. At least for us in the West. We, too, can move in a different direction, avoiding the Western forms of politics and economics, which are ruined and hollowed out but still hegemonic and once again represent a barrier to attempts to pursue real change.

I think the anti-artistic avant-garde groups, the communist ones, the Surrealists, the Situationists, Black Mask, and others already knew this. That is why they were avant-gardes without being vanguards in a political sense. They sought to unite revolutionary organisation with freedom. They were not Leninist cadres intent on leading the masses through a revolutionary upheaval. They did not see themselves as future rulers with five-year plans and political programmes. They were lost children playing with the dead forms of art and politics in an attempt to de-commodify everyday life. They had dedicated themselves to provoking and destroying the established order and were not in the business of leading anyone or telling the workers what to do.

A century on from the experiments of the Soviet avant-garde and the founding of the Surrealist group, I think we can see

---

20   Sylvia Wynter, "Columbus, the Ocean Blue, and Fables That Stir the Mind: To Reinvent the Study of Letters," Bainard Cowan and Jefferson Humphries (eds.), *Poetics of the Americas: Race, Founding, and Textuality* (Baton Rouge & London: Louisiana State University Press, 1997), 151.

that these groups sought to develop a complex solidarity that was still nascent at the time, but which is coming into its own in the form of a revolutionary postcolonial position today on the streets of Paris, Minneapolis, Teheran, and elsewhere. The artistic avant-gardes understood clearly, as few others did at the time, that colonial capitalism is one barbaric event after another. If the violence in the colonies had not already made this explicit, then World War One cemented for the Dadaists, the Constructivists, and the Surrealists that Western civilisation is founded on and compelled to reproduce itself through enormous amounts of state terror: From the 'discovery' of America to New Echota to Congo to Verdun to Auschwitz to Hiroshima onwards. In the far-flung colonies and in the centres of capital, state terror was the order of the day. This is why they looked elsewhere and sought inspiration in practices and life forms deemed backwards by European modernity. There is no doubt that the primitivism of the avant-gardes was characterised by exoticism, but they sought to become barbarians in order to escape the prison of state and capital.

Modernisation and Style as Counter-Revolution

When the revolution did not take place, the avant-garde was transformed into modernisation and style, shorthand for Le Corbusier and Dali, respectively. This happened to both the inter-war avant-gardes and the few desperate gestures after World War Two. The dream landscapes and grotesque figures of Surrealism, in which wo/men and animals melted together or disintegrated, quickly turned into cliches that made it fairly easy for the film and advertising industries to put Surrealist motives to work. As Manfredo Tafuri put it in one of the bleakest readings of the avant-garde: negation was repurposed as feedback in the cybernetic network of post-war planner capitalism.[21] The Situationists sought desperately to learn the lessons of the past taking two steps backwards every time they intervened in existing institutions. They preferred obscurity to five minutes of fame, but nonetheless, their contribution to a radical capital-negating critique ended up as part of a standardised market for individual dependency, in which the production of identity is a zero-sum game no one can ever escape. There is no outside. As Benjamin puts it in his fragment on capitalism as religion, every day is a feast day from which the worshipper cannot escape.[22] "I Like me," as it says in the shop window.

European avant-gardes played a significant role in the history of the critique of institutions and ideas of Euro-modernity, short-circuiting all the sovereigntist phantasies. There is no doubt that their explicit anti-nationalism and anti-colonialism remain forms of frugal primitivism, which it is necessary to make strategic[23], but their radical self-critique is nonetheless a good starting point for any kind of radical action today that strives to affirm our collective incompleteness.[24]

For us Westerners, this struggle includes a fight against the I. As André Breton put it, Rimbaud and Marx were both

---

21   Manfredo Tafuri, *Architecture and Utopia: Design and Capitalist Development* [1973] (Cambridge, MA: MIT Press, 1979).

22   Walter Benjamin, "Capitalism as Religion" 1921], *Selected Writings. Volume I: 1913-1926*, 288.

23   "Strategic primitivism" is Eduardo Viveiros de Castro's formulation. "For a Strategic Primitivism: A Dialogue between Eduardo Viverios de Castro and Yuk Hui," *Philosophy Today*, vol. 65, no. 2, 2021, 391-400

24   Stefano Harney and Fred Moten, *All Incomplete* (Colchester: Minor Compositions, 2021).

engaged in an attack on identity.[25] Rimbaud was another – *je est un autre* – and Marx conceptualised class struggle as the self-abolition of the proletariat, because the proletariat is not an identity to be affirmed, but the class destined to abolish class. In the revolution, all classes would disappear. The fight against identity is a constant in all the Euro-modernist avant-gardes. The Situationists were so preoccupied with the society of the spectacle in the 1960s precisely because they sought to continue the inter-war avant-garde's dismantling of all the dominant narratives surrounding humanity, not least the concept of the artist as creative genius.

Any attempt to return to the avant-garde requires a proviso or two because the meaning of avant-garde – both as a noun and adjective – seems to rest on the idea of progress. In both art and politics, such an idea has long since perished. The military metaphor of art marching at the forefront of society and of some artists being ahead of others has long ago fallen into disrepute. It is just extremely difficult to be the avant-garde of anything when nothing seems to move anywhere. Peter Osborne has recently analysed the coming together of different but equally present times without a future as "contemporaneity."[26] According to Osborne, we are confronted with a kind of blocked temporality caused by global capitalism or the globalisation of economic relations and their systems of communication. He stresses the element of cancelation that has occurred when it comes to the question of revolution. Unfortunately, however, he turns this situation into a general condition and seems to have no time for the anti-artistic practices or the many protests that actually still occur all over the place. No doubt the-

---

25   André Breton, "Speech to the Congress of Writers" [1935], *Manifestoes of Surrealism* (Ann Arbor: University of Michigan Press, 1969), 241.

26   Peter Osborne, *Anywhere or Not At All: Philosophy of Contemporary Art* (London & New York: Verso, 2013).

se protests form a discontinuous pattern without reference to previous historical ideas of political action, but nonetheless they contain a refusal, a process of experimentation that Osborne does not seem to consider to be of any value. Perhaps he is incapable of exiting the 20th century's dominant account of art (individual artworks that primarily thematise their own limits) and politics (democratic reforms of the state and its running of the economy), and therefore remains blind to all the different, admittedly convoluted and paradoxical gestures that point towards a different kind of political art, the "little narratives," from Kronstadt 1921 to the Sudan Commune in 2019, from the statue of Fourier at Place Clichy in 1969 to the amputation of Oñate's right foot in 1998.[27]

The avant-garde was one long, painful self-critique, in which the negative always ended up being laterally reversed and could always be re-inscribed within the positive logic of re-presentation. The rupture became continuity. Sublation was always preservation. Every time the artwork was negated, its concept was expanded. We cannot have a final complete

---

27   For an analysis of the action in 1998 where a group of Acoma Pueblo activists cut off the right foot of a statue of the Spanish conquistador Juan de Oñate y Salazar in front of the Oñate Monument and Visitor Centre in New Mexico, see Michael L. Trujillo, "Oñate's Foot: Remembering and Dismembering in Northern New Mexico," *Aztlán: A Journal of Chicano Studies*, vol. 33, no. 2, 2008, 91-119. In 1969 the Situationists re-installed a replica of the statue of Charles Fourier that had been removed during World War Two under the German occupation. For a short presentation, see the account by the Situationists in the last issue of *Internationale situationniste*, nr. 12, 1969, 97-98. Debord describes the action in a letter to the Italian section dated the March 12th. Guy Debord, *Correspondance. Volume 4, 1969-1972* (Paris: Fayard, 2005), 42. François de Beaulieu, who participated in the action, talks about it in an interview with Christophe Bourseiller, "L'homme est un homme pour l'homme," *Archives & Documents situationnistes*, no. 3, 2003, 17-25. For an analysis that considers both actions, see Gene Ray's two texts, "Ode to an Empty Plinth: Iconoclasm by Other Means" and "Justice Afoot: Communing with the Friends of Acoma," *Issue: Journal of Art and Design HEAD Genève*, no. 8, 2021, https://issue-journal. ch/focus-summaries/issue-8-all-monuments-must-fall/.

theory of the artistic avant-garde because it will never manage to overcome itself, and yet it constantly tries to realise art in everyday life, which inevitably ends up confirming that art exists in a world of separations.

The paradox of the avant-garde's radical gesture of transgression is that it inevitably occurs at the exact moment it is supposed to be replaced by a different kind of supersession. The realisation of art is thus always already suspended. Phrased in a 'post-structuralist' fashion, we could say that it is always coming or yet to come. For the avant-garde, there was nothing positive about this state of affairs, about the suspended nature of radical critique. The more desperately the avant-garde sought to overcome itself, the more it made itself present. By necessity, the realisation of art in everyday life took the form of an artistic gesture or experience.

The Situationists' critique of Surrealism was so high-pitched because they knew full well that they were trapped in the paradox of negative dialectics, where the supersession is constantly posited but never happens. The only thing left after the end of art is the critical position, but whenever established taste is attacked and ridiculed, the attack assumes a new value. This was the conclusion of the Italian post-Situationist avant-garde theoreticians in the early and mid-1970s. As Giorgio Agamben put it in 1977, in the push to abolish art by realising it, the Situationists paradoxically ended up extending it to the entirety of human existence.[28] Mario Perniola arrived at the same conclusion after having spent some time on the periphery of the Situationist group in the late 1960s.[29] However, as

---

28   Giorgio Agamben, *Stanzas: Word and Phantasm in Western Culture* [1977] (Minneapolis: University of Minnesota Press, 1993), p. 54.

29   Mario Perniola, *I situazionisti. Il movimento che ha profetizzato la 'Società dello spettacolo'* [1972] (Rome: Castelvecchi, 1998).

he noted, the Situationists had been among the few groups who actually understood that since the late 1950s a revolt had been underway among migrants, the racialised, young people, and in the colonies. A process that culminated in May '68 in France and in Italy in 1977, but also included subaltern militant movements in the former colonies, 'apolitical' riots in Watts, Detroit and Seattle, as well as huge protests behind the Iron Curtain. The Situationists understood that the revolution entailed a different kind of subjectivity beyond the avant-garde itself and its nonsensical monopoly on criticism. The revolution would take place on the streets and it would have to be the work of "unknown and nameless authors," according to Raoul Vaneigem.[30]

As the vast number of exclusions and the split in the International showed, the Situationists never really managed to come to terms with this understanding of the revolutionary process: They somehow kept believing that they were the absolute subject. The Situationist International was the last avant-garde, the culmination of Euro-modernity and its self-critique, at one and the same time the apotheosis and negation of the Western subject. The affirmation of the dream of the free individual as well as the self-murder of that notion. The avant-garde as the negation of the West by itself.

The Class Politics of the Avant-Garde, or the Context of the Avant-Garde

The avant-garde was the space where modern art came closest to living up to its anti-systemic perspective, willing to risk everything, including art itself, in an effort to abolish its great enemy,

---

30   Raoul Vaneigem, *The Revolution of Everyday Life* [1967] (Oakland: PM Press, 2012), 46.

capitalism. The avant-garde was not only an attempt to inhabit capital's intense and overwhelming destruction of all inherited relations but also to critique the different re-territorialisations capital came up with along the way – the nation state, property, the family, the individual, the individual's identity – institutions and authorities that all confirm the inevitability of the capital-labour relationship and capitalist society. The avant-garde wanted to create a different world beyond capitalism, "the inevitable liquidation of the world of privation, in all its forms."[31] The artwork as an event, as a revolutionary break, "a constructed situation," the magic circle Johan Huizinga writes about, in which the infernal "oscillation between the reactionary paranoiac overcharges and the subterranean, schizophrenic, and revolutionary charges" is broken.[32] Hence the alliance and collaboration with Communism in its different forms. Communism not as state capitalism, bureaucracy and gulags, as became the case from the late 1920s in the Soviet Union, but as the project of a liberation of human needs from any kind of determination – what Marx called "a higher form of socialism" when everybody would live without money or programme.

This was the avant-garde as a desperate effort to affirm the new life produced by the Moloch of capital. Affirm it, but differently, without the oppressive re-territorialisations. Not settling for the hollowing-out, by means of which previous ideas and socialities lose their meaning, but trying to find a new and different meaning in all the madness. And an attack on the new disorder of capital, in which profit and destruction fuse in

---

31   The Situationist International, "Situationist Manifesto" [1960], Mikkel Bolt Rasmussen and Jakob Jakobsen (eds.), *Cosmonauts of the Future: Texts from the Situationist Movement in Scandinavia and Elsewhere* (Copenhagen: Nebula, 2015), 49.

32   Gilles Deleuze and Félix Guattari, *Anti-Oedipus: Capitalism and Schizophrenia* [1972] (Minneapolis: University of Minnesota Press, 1983), 260.

an open-ended circuit, meaningless, beyond the ever-constant production of surplus value. In other words, the avant-garde as the search for a meaning beyond the invisible hand of the market. A romantic anti-capitalist gesture that necessitates a revolutionary critique of capitalist society.

This was the perspective formulated most succinctly by the small Situationist group in the early 1960s. However, Breton, Naville, Debord, and Nash are no longer with us. The best thing to do would probably be to follow Perniola, Tafuri and Peter Bürger. As Bürger puts it in his classic 1974 book, written on the heels of the breakdown of the West German student opposition that he indirectly links to the avant-gardes: "But it is a historical fact that the avant-garde movements did not put an end to the production of works of art, and that the social institution that is art proved resistant to the avant-gardist attack. The revival of art as an institution and the revival of the category 'work' suggest that today, the avant-garde is already historical."[33] That the avant-garde, in other words, is dead.

In a specific historical period, artists sought to transcend modern art ideology by scandalising both the institution of art and the norms of the emerging bourgeois society by giving art a function in a transformed and re-enchanted Communist everyday life. In 1974, six years after May '68 in Paris and Mexico City, Bürger concluded that the project had failed – that the heroic push by the inter-war avant-gardes had been replaced by "the farcical repetitions" of the neo-avant-garde that turned Dada and Surrealism into gestures internal to the world of art.

Bürger presents the avant-garde as a heroic historical project in the inter-war years, but which was absorbed in a farcical

---

33   Peter Bürger, *Theory of the Avant-Garde* [1974] (Minneapolis: University of Minnesota Press, 1984), 56-57.

fashion by the different artistic practices in the booming post-war era, from Pop to Fluxus onwards. We can – post-Bürger – expand his rather limited internal historical analysis of art and say that the avant-garde was a historical phenomenon that emerged in tandem with the early 20th-century revolutionary movements, attacking the aesthetic practices of the old regime and the emerging bourgeoisie alike, with a view to bringing forth a new world. This project failed, and as 'free experimental art,' the avant-garde was integrated into booming post-war modernising cultures, in which culture and symbolic production played an important role in a new accumulation regime. This is the story of a shift from a revolutionary anti-artistic perspective to the simulacrum of the same, from a full-frontal attack on the institution of art to institutional acceptance, from self-critical experiments of the revolutionary breakthrough outside the institutions of modern capitalist society to the aesthetics of advertising. This is a history of decline, in which the early 1970s would represent the obvious end point of the history of the avant-garde.

Debord and Sanguinetti dissolved the small Situationist group in 1972. Debord summed up the situation six years later: "Avant-gardes have only one time; and the best thing that can happen to them is to have enlivened their time without *outliving* it. After them, operations move onto a vaster terrain."[34] Bürger's short avant-garde book was published in 1974. At that point, Perniola had already discussed the inherent contradictions of the avant-garde position in a series of articles in *Agaragar*, in which he noted that the negative element was always mystified and presented as a conciliated vision of the opposite of existing reality. Then, in 1975, Manfredo Tafuri rewrote his 1969 article "Per una critica dell'Ideologia

---

34   Guy Debord, *In girum imus nocte et consumimur igni* [1978], *Not Bored*, 2002,
     http://www.bopsecrets.org/SI/debord.films/ingirum.htm

architettonica" as *Progetto e utopia,* hammering the final nail in the coffin of the avant-garde. For Tafuri, the problem was not that the avant-garde had ended up in the museum, betrayed by the neo-avant-garde, but that the avant-garde had, from the get-go, misunderstood its role. Its anti-artistic experiments could never in themselves transcend capitalist modernisation. The avant-garde "came into being, developed, and entered into crisis as an enormous attempt – the last to be made by the great bourgeois artistic culture – to resolve, on the always more outdated level of ideology, the imbalances, contradictions, and retardations characteristic of the capitalist reorganisation of the world market and productive development," Tafuri concluded.[35]

The lesson here is pretty straightforward. By the mid-1970s, during the repurposing and recuperation after May '68, the avant-garde finally disappeared, if indeed it hadn't already been gone since World War Two, as Bürger and Tafuri both argued. It might be best, after all, to make do with the notion of the avant-garde as a designation of a specific period. Confronted with art critics and art historians who, in the most clichéd fashion, invoke the avant-garde when analysing and promoting institutionally sanctioned and attention-seeking late fascist artworks, such as Mathieu Malouf's *Tankie Meme (Blacked),* as avant-gardist provocations it might be better to simply ditch the term and accept that the avant-garde is really dead and gone.

On the other hand, if we totally relinquish the idea of the avant-garde, we downgrade artistic practice to such an extent that it more or less necessarily fuses with its autonomy as an imagined averted gesture while being in reality part and parcel

---

35   Manfredo Tafuri, *Architecture and Utopia: Design and Capitalist Development,* 178.

of the unending hollowing out of human imagination – i.e. autonomy and its dissolution (in the Spectacle) as two seemingly opposed movements both confirming the alienation of capitalist society. Abstraction and separation, as Debord would say.

No matter how we readjust our understanding of the avant-garde, it appears to be a thing of the past, and we know all the charges as well as the case for the defence. We have been here before. It is difficult not to feel a certain sense of déjà vu, if not outright fatigue, when it comes to the discussion of the existence, meaning, and disappearance of the avant-garde. Do we really have to keep talking about it?

It may seem tiresome to return to the question of the avant-garde for the umpteenth time and compare it with later and contemporary artistic practices trying to locate an avant-garde, or at least the semblance of one, for example, analysing the meaning of the presence of anti-artistic gestures in contemporary art that questions the function of art, when institutional critique is now a standard institutional requirement in itself; or comparing the naivety of the avant-garde's confrontational attack on the conventions of bourgeois society with the subtlety (or is it banality?) of contemporary art. Was the avant-garde, in the end, merely a test- and development unit for the market, always ready to expand and subsume ever-new areas and spheres of human life?

Conditions of Impossibility

In two long analyses of the terms modernism and postmodernism, the first a discussion of Marshall Berman's magnum opus *All that is Solid Melts into Air*, the second a book-length discussion of Fredric Jameson's texts on postmodernism, Perry Anderson offers a useful stab at sketching the historical conjuncture of the avant-garde movements.[36] As Anderson writes, Berman's account of modernism as the translation into artistic form of the experience of modernity and the process of capitalist modernisation tends to homogenise different episodes or eras and misses the differential temporality of the capitalist mode of production, in which eras are discontinuous from each other and heterogenous within themselves. Modernist art has to be explained conjuncturally, Anderson writes, by analysing the intersection of different historical temporalities as an overdetermined configuration. What Anderson calls modernism (his examples are Italian Futurism and German Expressionism) was triangulated by three coordinates: an open political horizon where the established order appeared, if not doomed, then at least challenged by different new ideologies, a roaring technological development that seemed to promise a completely new life, and the continued presence of old aristocratic regimes' and their cultural and political forms.[37] Referencing Arno Mayer's *The Persistence of the Old Regime*, Anderson writes that avant-garde modernism was confronted with a highly formalised academicism that it could ridicule. This academicism was, of course, itself the cultural expression of the presence of an old aristocratic elite not yet politically replaced by the bourgeoisie. However, these elites were obviously losing ground, hence the open political horizon where the dream or nightmare of a social revolution loomed large. It was 'in the air' threatening the still-lingering monarchies or empires in Germany, Italy, Russia and Austria, as well as in the United Kingdom and many other European states. From the 'left,' the working-class movement threatened a crisis-ridden capital that was reluctant to afford the workers' movement

---

36   Perry Anderson, "Modernity and Revolution" [1984], *A Zone of Engagement* (London & New York: Verso, 1992), 25-55; and idem, *The Origins of Postmodernity* (London & New York: Verso, 1998).

37   Perry Anderson, "Modernity and Revolution," 34-36.

a political and social role. The working class did not try to overthrow bourgeois rule in Western Europe after 1921, but the ruling order nonetheless remained in a state of panic, constantly afraid of unions and political parties and, even more, the invisible organisation of the dangerous classes. It took two world wars for capital to accept the labouring class and its representatives as a junior political partner in the running of capital. The first half of the 20th century was one long civil war with interstate conflicts and a ruthless confrontation between a militant working class and a bourgeoisie unsure of itself, alternating between repressing or integrating workers, all the while also removing the last vestiges of the old order. This was the context for the avant-garde. Anderson paints a convincing picture of a set of specific circumstances that made possible the avant-garde's radical gesture, and his analysis helps us contextualise Bürger's, Perniola's, and Tafuri's 'internal' readings from the world of art.

The conclusion from Anderson's 1984 sketch of the origins of the avant-garde and its conjunctural triangulation seems to be pretty clear. The avant-garde emerged and disappeared in the tumultuous decades at the beginning of the 20th century, in the period that historians like Mayer, Enzo Traverso, and right-wing historian Ernst Nolte have all called "the European civil war."[38] This is also Anderson's conclusion from his analysis of Jameson's postmodernism thesis, in which he updates his reading of Berman. The Berman piece was written in the early 1980s, and the analysis of Jameson's works is from the late 1990s. The intermediate years seem only to have confirmed Anderson's initial periodisation. As he puts it in the book

---

38   Arno Mayer, *Why Did the Heavens Not Darken? The 'Final Solution' in History* (New York: Pantheon Books, 1988); Ernst Nolte, *The Three Faces of Fascism* [1963] (London: Weidenfeld & Nicolson, 1965); Enzo Traverso, *Fire and Blood: The European Civil War, 1914-1945* [2007] (London & New York: Verso, 2016).

from 1998: "The caesura came with the Second World War."[39] The war not only united the classes of each country in the trenches, but also effectively removed the old agrarian elites from the political scene. After 1945, national democracy united the people, including the working class, as one nation. The revolutionary fervour of the inter-war years slowly evaporated or became stuck in the Cold War opposition between East and West, two opposing capitalist systems that both understood revolution as modernisation and industrialised standardisation. The ideals of revolution were gutted in the East and took on the form of consumer durables in the West, as Anderson writes.

Anderson largely follows Jameson's analysis of the emergence of postmodernism and argues that the avant-garde did not disappear overnight, but lived on ghost-like in the field of art. The conditions were no longer there, but some of the strategies and tactics of the avant-garde persisted for a period. The radical gesture was still there in Abstract Expressionism, randomness was still a principle in Fluxus, and in the late 1950s the ready-made returned big time in Pop Art. The avant-garde as a group and organisation, to a certain extent, remained a model, at least in the old art centre, Paris, but never really managed to make it to New York. However, it was only a question of time, and the phenomenon of Abstract Expressionism showed the inescapability of "commercial integration" and "institutional co-option."[40]

In retrospect, the whole postmodernism debate now sounds very strange. For some, like Jean-François Lyotard, it was an attempt to question the historical logic of historical materialism with a view to saving a radical analysis of differences. For others, like Alex Callinicos, it was not only a reactionary

---

39   Perry Anderson, *The Origins of Postmodernity*, 82.

40   Ibid., 82.

attack on materialist analyses of capitalist society but also a political attempt to legitimate a shift to the right.[41] Jameson's analysis was interesting because it sought to follow Lyotard while remaining solidly Marxist. Lyotard had argued that grand-scale historical analyses of the Marxist kind were no longer possible.[42] The information society that was emerging could not be analysed using references to class struggle, he argued. They were too complex, as he wrote in his famous report written on behalf of the Quebec universities in the late 1970s.

Jameson took up the term, prefacing the translation of Lyotard's book into English, but contrary to Lyotard, sought to use it to describe a period. The postmodern condition of Lyotard became postmodernism as a cultural logic for Jameson.[43] Postmodern was a description of an era that made a historical Marxist analysis difficult but not impossible, contrary to what Lyotard had argued. Jameson thus sought to bridge the widening gap between the limited perspective of the individual subject and the totality of the economic structure, in which the subject was caught. The title of his notorious article and later book underscored this attempt: "Postmodernism, or, the Cultural Logic of Late Capitalism."

The challenge was to conduct historical analysis at a moment when the historical seemed to become opaque, and a number of the central notions of capitalist modernity were becoming

---

41   Alex Callinicos, *Against Postmodernism: A Marxist Critique* (Cambridge: Polity, 1991).

42   Jean- François Lyotard, *The Postmodern Condition: A Report on Knowledge* [1979] (Minneapolis: University of Minnesota Press, 1984).

43   Fredric Jameson, *Postmodernism, or, The Cultural Logic of Late Capitalism* (London: Verso, 1992).

obsolete.[44] This was the case with the notion of class, but also other concepts like ideology, art, and social democracy.[45] Jameson nonetheless persisted and used the Trotskyist Ernst Mandel's analysis of a new third, late phase in the development of capital as a framework for his own reading of late capitalism's cultural logic – postmodernism.

Jameson's object was the new cultural and aesthetic production that had emerged, characterised by a particular subjectivity and temporality. The subject of postmodernism was a free-floating, de-centred and fragmented non-self, he wrote. Jameson's work was, in many ways, an attempt to update an analysis of capitalist society and its cultural forms inspired by Critical Theory at a time when that was no longer possible. Adorno had used the term "late capitalism" in the 1960s in tandem with the notion of a "class-less class society." Jameson followed suit with his postmodernism thesis, although the relationship between political-economic and cultural periodisation is slightly off-kilter in Jameson's *late* and *post*. In retrospect, the choice of *post* seems somewhat strange but can be understood as a gesture aimed at upholding the prospect of a post-capitalist world at a moment when capital had assumed a near-triumphant and neo-evangelic tone. When the book version of Jameson's text appeared in 1991, two years after the fall of the Berlin Wall, revolution was more or less reduced to Stalin or Pol Pot.

Jameson's analysis may be somewhat homogenising, but he is at pains to describe the shift as a gradual and open

---

44   Jameson defined the task as an attempt to "think the present historically in an age that has forgotten how to think historically." Ibid., IX.

45   "The last few years have been marked by an inverted millenarianism in which premonitions of the future, catastrophic or redemptive, have been replaced by senses of the end of this or that (the end of ideology, art, or social class; the 'crisis' of Leninism, social democracy, or the welfare state, etc., etc.)." Ibid., 1.

development, meaning that postmodernism should be understood as a "force field in which very different kinds of cultural impulses – what Raymond Williams has usefully termed 'residual' and 'emergent' forms of cultural production – must make their way."[46] Postmodernism was not a description of all cultural production but "a dominant cultural logic" that was rapidly becoming hegemonic.[47]

Central to Jameson's account was, of course, the waning of critical distance and the disappearance of feelings. The cultural logic of late capitalism was distinguished by the crumbling of historicity and references that amount to a significant shift because it means that it is the very capacity to lose that is lost. To lose something means there is something to lose in the first place. This was no longer the case. It was becoming more and more difficult to locate the loss, both temporally and spatially.

Jameson concluded that the postmodern subject was, therefore, no longer in any meaningful sense alienated because there was no interiority to which to refer. The subject had become fragmented in a different way than the modern alienation described by Simmel and German sociology. The dialectics between interior and exterior in a painting like Munch's "The

---

46   Ibid., p. 6.

47   Jameson has since sought to update his analysis from 1992, but has until recently more or less consistently kept the term (most other participants rather quickly moved away from it). In later texts, Jameson has mainly supplemented Mandel's analysis of the third technological revolution with the analysis of the Italian world-system theoretician Giovanni Arrighi from his *The Long Twentieth Century*, in which Arrighi presents a geopolitical analysis of the development of capital from the late Middle Ages to "the short American century." He maps a series of long centuries during which the combination of state and market drove the accumulation of capital from expansion to financial speculation. This enables Jameson to include globalisation and financialisation in his later analysis of postmodernity. However, the overall coordinates – outlining a shift from modernity to postmodernity – remain the same.

Scream" was replaced by "a strange, compensatory, decorative exhilaration" in Warhol's "Diamond Dust Shoes." Referencing Lacan and Baudrillard, Jameson described this as the emergence of a culture of simulacrum, in which the signifying chain breaks down, resulting in a fractured self that moves from one disconnected event to the next. This amounts to a kind of ever-extended present, where it is difficult to connect the present with a past and a future.

As the matter at hand is the avant-garde and its status today, I will not delve further into Jameson's analysis of postmodernism. The point of including Jameson is, of course, that post-modernism means the disappearance of the avant-garde and the avant-garde perspective. As Jameson puts it in *Postmodernism, or, The Cultural Logic of Late Capitalism*, postmodernism arrives when the avant-garde becomes a "structural impossibility."[48]

Traditional avant-gardes and collective movements have become impossible, he writes. The restructuring of capital, the transition to the third phase analysed by Mandel, erased the context of the avant-garde. Any continuity in the inter-war period had been broken by the reorganisation of capital. In the metropoles of capitalist accumulation, class conflict seemed to have disappeared, and an enormous number of representations circulated by powerful new machines of symbolisation papered over the existing cracks. The structural violence of capital moved to the margins of the world system.

This is postmodernism as the erosion of the conditions of possibility of the avant-garde, as Perry Anderson writes. The three-fold transformation that effectively closed the door to the avant-garde's radical perspective: The narrowing of the political horizon, the evident damage caused by new

---

48   Ibid., 184-185.

technology– the industrialised mass death of war and death camps – and the ruling bourgeoisie's gradual fade to invisibility. The avant-garde had emerged in a context in which competing ideologies fought for the right to create a new world and new technologies would facilitate those visions. This was simply no longer the case, Jameson and Anderson concluded. The postmodernism thesis is an analysis of the closing of the historical space in which modern art gradually downscales its self-critique and embraces the market as a premise for the production and reception of art experiences. As Jameson puts it, referring to Anderson's discussion of Berman, "the deepest and most fundamental feature" of avant-garde modernism was "hostility to the market itself. The centrality of this feature is then confirmed by its inversion in the various postmodernisms."[49]

Jameson and Anderson reaffirm the analyses put forth in the 1970s by Bürger and Tafuri, in which the bad dream of modernism has become real: the project of the avant-garde has been realised upside down through the integration of art and commodity production. This is, of course, a story we already know, from Adorno and Horkheimer and Marcuse and Debord, among others. Jameson's postmodernism thesis is an attempt to update these analyses of how art loses its once critical potential. For Bürger, Tafuri and Jameson, the only critical position left is their own, that of the Marxist critic, who can somehow still point to a missing totality.

Break or Continuity

We seem to have circled back to the beginning, or the end, the disappearance of the avant-garde. Crisis and breakdown. Not that the art institution is not thriving, it is, but as a mere

---

49   Ibid., 304-305.

shadow of the potential it was supposed to imbue: an internal/external challenge and testing ground of the differentiation of capitalist modernity. Contemporary art also curates politically and represents socio-political struggles, but the institution has integrated all of that. The curator has replaced the avant-garde and stages temporary events. The history of the avant-garde is definitely over.

The avant-garde modernist story of the avant-garde's decline is highly convincing. There are obviously differences between, say, Tafuri and Bürger, Debord and Jameson. There is a historical agency in Debord that moves history, which probably makes it easier to abandon art. The proletariat is also still present in Debord, and to some extent in Tafuri as well, although in the guise of a proletariat embedded in a party structure, which Debord abhors. For Adorno and Jameson, the classless class society has taken on the appearance of eternity, and the proletariat is nowhere to be seen. Debord continued elsewhere, conspiring. Tafuri puts his faith in the class analysis of culture, demystifying architecture. Not unlike Bürger, who is also left with a historical analysis but in his case of disappearance, not misrecognition as in Tafuri.

Perhaps it is fitting that we continue to go round and round in circles. This might actually tell us something about the matter at hand – that the crisis is constitutive, that the death of the avant-garde has been there all along, that the avant-garde is always necessarily in crisis and necessarily recuperated, always disappearing. This was the case as far back as the inter-war period. The situation has always been one of acceleration. The lengthy list of rows and exclusions says it all. The avant-garde murders itself attempting to produce a new world, fighting a superior power that is using the avant-garde's small gesture of revolt in ever-new moves towards capitalist de-territorialisation. It has always been too late. The avant-garde has always been in a hurry, time is of the essence, the political horizon is always closing, the revolutionary launch pad is always being used by counter-revolutionary forces.

No one would deny that we have powerful image machines at our disposal today that the Surrealists could never have imagined. It is also difficult to compare the art institution of the 1920s to the experience economy art is part and parcel of today. However, the spectacle is not exactly a new phenomenon. This is why Debord does not date the spectacle. It is, so to speak, a constitutive condition that confronted Baudelaire and Rimbaud back in their day and something Tzara, Ball, and Jacques Rigault were also up against. The end was rapidly approaching for all of them. Berman is right to stress the dizzying character of capitalist modernity. "Constant revolutionizing of production, uninterrupted disturbance of all social conditions, everlasting uncertainty and agitation distinguish the bourgeois epoch from all earlier ones. All fixed, fast-frozen relations, with their train of ancient and venerable prejudices and opinions, are swept away, all new-formed ones become antiquated before they can ossify. All that is solid melts into air."[50] Capital as a "polymorph perversity" and diabolic force that trashes life forms and routines as it opens new markets.[51]

The avant-garde was engaged in a fierce battle with this Moloch. This was what gave it its apocalyptic dimension. It ripped off the avant-garde that both sought to accelerate the destructive processes and equip the negation with a new meaning, to find some kind of meaning in the madness. "The problem now

---

50   Karl Marx and Friedrich Engels, *Manifesto of the Communist Party* [1848], marxist.org, https://www.marxists.org/archive/marx/works/1848/communist-manifesto/

51   Jean-François Lyotard described the polymorph perversity of capital in his analysis of Marx's difficulty of coming up with a definitive reading of the capitalist mode of production. Lyotard, *Libidinal Economy* [1974] (Bloomington: Indiana University Press, 1993), 2.

was that of teaching that one is not to 'suffer' that shock, but to absorb it as an inevitable condition of existence"[52] – coping with the shock of the metropolis and the insanely intense liquidation of traditions. Using the destruction as a starting point. The avant-garde often mistook capital for the bourgeoisie and ridiculed it, scandalising its pretentious norms and self-aggrandising self-representations that often imitated the old order's forms. However, the avant-garde, more often than not, engaged in a real critique of money and the fundamental categories of capital, such as work and the commodity. Naturally, in some of these instances, the critique ended up in an abandonment of art as a separate practice.

What I'm saying is that the ending has been ongoing from the start, that the avant-garde is always already dead. This would be one way of reading all the 'the avant-garde is in crisis' stories. The conditions of possibility of the avant-garde have really always been conditions of impossibility. At which moment was the political horizon not in the process of closing? Was the Third International not a derailment of revolutionary energy? When has the art institution and the established taste not flirted with radical gestures and used them somehow? As a movement, revolutionary opposition to capitalism had disappeared a few years before the Surrealist movement came into being. It was not at the end of World War Two and the emergence of the booming post-war economy that the avant-gardes became *enfants perdus* and faced difficulty enrolling in an organised revolutionary movement. This was already the case between the two great wars. The counter-revolutionary dynamic and the swiftness of the recuperation have no doubt been speeded up, but Heartfield and Grosz had to deal with it in Berlin in the 1920s, too, just as Bernstein and Debord had to in Paris in the 1950s.

---

52   Manfredo Tafuri, *Architecture and Utopia*, 86.

In retrospect, the resemblance between the anti-works of the avant-garde and the playful experiments of the neo-avant-garde is quite striking. The surface Jameson notes in Warhol's silkscreen pictures is an abstraction that has been there all along. The hollowing out is constitutive. Today Warhol's "Diamond Dust Shoes" look like Surrealist relics, the fashion objects of yesterday isolated and shown as part of an avant-gardist operation of *Verfremdung*. A sort of class analysis. Executed with the same kind of coolness as when Heartfield took a photo of the successful author Emil Ludwig and his family and used it as the book jacket for the German translation of Upton Sinclair's *Money Writes*, but due to legal problems had to blur the faces of the Ludwig family and resorted to simply cutting out the faces from the photos (including the family dog).[53] Or perhaps just as naively and handmade, cut and paste, the same bourgeois fascination and distaste for the new images we find in Debord's meticulously crafted film stills.[54]

Programmes

The argument is now that the avant-garde was impossible to begin with. Or that it emerged as this impossibility, a particular affirmation of the crisis of capitalist modernity. That from the get-go it fought a sovereign power it kept misperceiving, the nation, capital, the state, art, etc. The avant-garde is so busy it barely appears before it has to disappear again. This is a dark version of Berman's modernism. I have managed to zoom out to such an extent that capitalist modernity ends up

---

53   For an excellent analysis of the book jacket, see Devin Fore, *Realism after Modernism: The Rehumanization of Art and Literature* (Cambridge, MA & London: MIT Press, 2012), 277-281.

54   Cf. Fabien Danesi, Fabrice Flahutez and Emmanuel Guy, *La fabrique du cinema de Guy Debord* (Paris: Actes Sud, 2013).

becoming the condition of possibility of the revolutionary self-critique of the avant-garde. In other words, I am back at a Marxist version of the classical modernist idea of art's critical potential, where art is an alienated activity and where to use Perniola's rendering, art's free ideas without social efficiency are mirrored by the unfree efficiency of capitalist economy.

The damage this move incurs is evident: The distinction between modernism and avant-garde tends to disappear, and the distinction between historical and neo-avant-garde is lost. Have I ended up arguing that modernity was postmodern, that Jameson's endings have been going on from the start?

It is probably better to try and come up with a historical analysis. Yet another one, but one that does not internalise the postmodern end-of-history concept as the disappearance of class struggle, as paradoxically, Jameson and Osborne do. We need to retain a notion of a break.

Let the last word go to the French left communist group Théorie Communiste (TC). This small post-Situationist group has developed an interesting analysis of what it terms the programmatism of the workers' movement, in which the proletariat of a certain period emerged as an autonomous entity struggling to realise itself and abolish capitalism.

Théorie Communiste analyses history as cycles of struggle, in which the relation between capital and labour changes from the beginning of the 18th century onwards. The latest phase starts in the 1970s: TC describes this as the second phase of real subsumption. In the phase of formal subsumption and the first phase of real subsumption, class struggle was conceived as a struggle between two opposing classes around the right to lead capitalist society on the basis of class identity, be it bourgeois or proletarian. This is what they call programmatism, where the proletariat was conceived as the positive part of the class antagonism that could abolish the opposition between capital and labour. The revolution was the self-affirmation of the proletariat. "The dissolution of the contradiction is given as one side of the opposition," as Roland Simon puts it.[55] The activity of the specific class was a programme to be realised. The task was to emancipate the working class from the bourgeoisie and the disastrous effects of exploitation. The workers had their own culture or morals that should be allowed to reach their own fulfilment, above and beyond the alienation of capitalist social relationships.

The two dominant versions of Marxist revolutionary practice in the 20th century, namely social democracy and Leninism, subscribed to the idea of the proletariat's uncontaminated self-creation. Although different, they both conceived of class struggle as a question of liberating the essence of the proletariat from the mediations of capital. The means to this end diverged: whether the revolution was to take the form of a state coup and the dictatorship of the proletariat, parliamentary politics, the council, a period of transition or self-management, the proletariat was by nature revolutionary, and its labour was the real motive behind human history and should be unshackled from capitalist exploitation.

According to TC, this programme has become obsolete. The structural transformations that have taken place since the 1970s have changed the relationship between capital and labour, and the programmatist perspective has broken down. The wide-scale changes we often discuss under the unfortunate heading of 'neoliberal globalisation' – outsourcing and the spread of production to a global labour market, financialisation, the introduction of new technologies and the growth

---

55   Roland Simon, *Fondements critiques d'une théorie de la révolution. Au-delà de l'affirmation du prolétariat* (Marseilles: Senonevero, 2001), 5.

of precarious work – have resulted in the dissolution of the identity of the worker. The objective breakdown of the class relation (exclusion, slum and informal work, precarity, and deregulation) has a 'subjective' dimension: the collapse of antagonistic class politics.

Class opposition is no longer reproduced in the same way as before, nor is there an organic working-class culture to emancipate. In the present cycle, the working class is confronted with its own self-abolition. Previous notions of a 'socialisation of production' or the establishment of a 'dictatorship of the proletariat 'no longer make sense. This breakdown constitutes the bankruptcy of the established workers' movement in the Western World: The European Social Democratic parties and the large unions are all in deep crisis, and even the financial meltdown of 2007–2008 proved incapable of reviving them or breathing new life into old shibboleths. There is no New Deal, no NEP, to manage.

Today, proletarian self-affirmation, no matter what form it might take, is a dead end. "The class activity of the proletariat is more and more torn in an internal way: as long as it remains the action of a class, it has capital as its sole horizon (because all liberation of work and affirmation of the proletariat as the dominant class have disappeared), simultaneously in its action against capital it is its own existence as a class that it faces and that it must treat as something to do away with."[56] TC's conclusion is clear: the transition to the second phase of real subsumption has destroyed the conditions of possibility that were still available in previous era's political forms: In the national democratic arena as well as the vanguard party, the unions, and the anti-artistic avant-garde we might add. If they

---

56   Théorie Communiste, "The Glass Floor" [2009], *libcom.org*, https://libcom.org/article/glass-floor-theo-cosme

continue to exist, it is as dead forms, devoid of the content and meaning they previously represented. It no longer makes sense to affirm the individual's status as a producer. The organisational forms of the first phase of real subsumption, what could be called the Fordist accumulation regime, have become hollow. The party-political form is finished, as is the union, and in the same breath, the avant-garde. The avant-garde was part of a specific historical period when the proletariat emerged as a class with its own particular identity and culture. During that period, the task of the avant-garde was to negate art as a specialised activity and make it available to all workers.

The avant-garde negated art, and itself as art, in order to liberate art's potential in everyday life as a realisation of Marx's dream of a complete individual who could go hunting in the morning, fishing in the afternoon and write poems in the evening – an end to the specialised activities of the capitalist commodity economy.[57] The avant-garde ended up trapped in the prison of art, forever ready to engage in the anti-artistic gesture that was supposed to finally realise art. Negation and realisation went hand in hand: everyday life into art (collage, montage, etc.) and art into a transformed everyday life (socialist objects, interventions), and the critique of everyday life (détournement, the constructed situation, etc.). The endless list of art-negating gestures that always ended up confirming art through its own negation. Art is dead, long live art!

---

57   "For as soon as the distribution of labor comes into being, each man has a particular exclusive sphere of activity, which is forced upon him and from which he cannot escape. He is a hunter, a fisherman, a herdsman, or a critical critic, and must remain so if he does not want to lose his means of livelihood; while in communist society, where nobody has one exclusive sphere of activity, but each can become accomplished in any branch he wishes, society regulates the general production and thus makes it possible for me to do one thing today and another tomorrow." Karl Marx and Friedrich Engels, *The German Ideology* [1846], *marxists.org*, https://www.marxists.org/archive/marx/works/1845/german-ideology/

We are again stuck with the Situationists, the last avant-garde. The anti-avant-garde that ends up turning the entire world into a *Gesamtkunstwerk*. The last international that abandoned art but became its own work of art. The Situationist avant-garde was the culmination of programmatism when the revolution was a total transformation realised by a subject at once both totally alienated and emancipated. In the revolutionary break, the proletariat "had to become what it already was." The end point of all the hard work, exclusions and fights was the realisation of the proletariat, the proletariat as creative art workers finally freed from the constraints of wage and labour and the institution. The avant-garde's programmatism was the idea of a realisation of art, the belief that the spectator had to be liberated and become a participant in a transformed everyday life where the separation between theory and practice was abolished.

If we follow TC, then we must conclude that the period of the avant-garde is over and was part of the cycle of programmatism, alongside the worker's movement, Communist parties, trade unionism, and self-management. We have exited that period, and class struggle appears different today. Class is an external limit and there is no programme to realise. The revolution does not involve the self-realisation of the worker. The socialist workers' movement has disappeared. As the late G. M. Tamás stressed (differentiating between a properly Marxist and a Rousseau-E.P. Thompson view of the working class), its making is not a revolutionary process [58]. The revolution is something different. This does not mean that labour is not still exploited, nor that surplus value is not continually extracted. But neither is the enemy an emerging bourgeoisie, akin to the one we find in Thomas Mann's *Buddenbrooks* or

---

58   G. M. Tamás, "Telling the Truth about Class," Leo Panitch & Colin Leys (eds.), *Socialist Register 2006: Telling the Truth* (London: Merlin Press, 2005), 228-268.

in Benjamin's *Das Passagen-Werk*, but rather a capitalism lacking either a bourgeoisie or a proletariat element at all. We no longer have two rival classes, each with its own culture and ideology, battling for capitalism or socialism.

Gegen ohne Für Avantgarde

So where to now? There are several potential ways to wind down this discussion. We could counter the argument about the end of programmatism and the underlying political-economic conditions by instead insisting on the possibility of a renewed avant-garde perspective. This would entail critiquing TC as being far too structuralist while stressing that real subsumption is not something that only recently emerged over the last four decades, having undoubtedly been a tendency as far back as the mid-18th century. The description of the objective and subjective relationships, the second phase of real subsumption, and the breakdown of the affirmation of workers' autonomy can prove overly deterministic, and even if we gradually zoom in again, it may well be the case that there are many more similarities between say, an artist in 1920s Berlin and one in contemporary Mumbai.

Introducing TC was supposed to provide a way of ridding us of the avant-garde without ditching a radical Communist perspective that poses the question of new political forms. The relation between capital and labour has changed: it pulled away the carpet beneath the party, as well as the avant-garde. The avant-garde turned out to be part of a cycle we have left behind. This fracture is often felt as a loss and a breakdown, but it will no doubt give rise to new forms. For the time being, however, it is difficult to spot the revolutionary potential in the struggles of today, not least in contemporary art. We are assailed by "non-movements."[59] However, this might be an occasion to finally affirm the breakdown of the workers' movement and the Western subject more generally, with a gentle nod to Mario Tronti.[60] Neither art nor the proletariat can be realised. Hounding the workers' movement and the avant-garde into the grave while developing new strategies that avoid reproducing the identities of capitalist Euro-modernity is the task of the next avant-garde. It will, by necessity, be an anonymous avant-garde. Its members will not show up and compete in positioning, be it this or that -ist (Communist, anarchist, socialist, Leninist). The next avant-garde will be an agency between individuality and singularity, a kind of nameless entity that is recognisable in the way it moves and talks and, most importantly, acts. It will be a different kind of mass movement, beyond seriality and crowd mentality, agile and adaptable, in order to remain in a position of confrontation.

A New Beginning?

The texts that constitute this small anthology speak for themselves. They are not in agreement as to what is to be done with the avant-garde, whether it is now finally a 'historical' problem we should primarily study meticulously or whether the avant-garde continues to be an important vehicle for progressive thought and action. As is evident from most of the titles, it is difficult to tackle the avant-garde head-on, it must be done tongue-in-cheque somehow. 'The avant-garde, now?'

---

59   As Endnotes argues, picking up the term from Asef Bayat. Endnotes, "Onward Barbarians," 2021, *Endnotes*, https://endnotes.org.uk/posts/endnotes-onward-barbarians

60   Mario Tronti, "Sul potere destituente. Discussione con Mario Tronti," Pierandrea Amato et al. (eds.), *Potere destituente. Le rivolte metropolitan* (Udine: Mimesis, 2008), 33-44.

But as is also evident from the texts the avant-garde continues to be more than a historical reference. It is difficult to let go of the avant-garde.

The texts come in two blocks; the first one, "Re-engaging with the Analysis of the Avant-Garde," gathers texts that aim at rereading the avant-garde in order to prevent it from ending up as a ready-made entity, always invoked but never really properly discussed or contextualised. We need to continue to excavate the ruins of avant-garde modernism, tracking and mapping heretofore neglected practices and groups, moving back and forth between a crisis-ridden present and the accelerated endings the avant-gardes lived through. The second block, "After the Avant-Garde," considers how we might best re-purpose the avant-garde in coming struggles, either by ditching the idea or adjusting it with a view to engage in a struggle of the possible meaning of 'culture.' This involves reflecting on the problem of the contemporary form of capitalist domination and the political or anti-political forms of opposition that are emerging in the present conjuncture. As will hopefully already be evident, the aim of this book is not to settle – as if that was even possible – the question of the avant-garde, but to keep it open and enquire what is left of the avant-garde today. We cannot complete the record of the avant-garde: this will be the work of the anonymous authors of the 'poetry of the future.'

Poetic Manifesto

Esther Leslie

The avant-garde is a corpse, when it is not a marketable prospect for some blockbuster exhibition at a major arts institution. But in that case, it is, as the saying goes, flogging a dead horse or, perhaps, flogging, in the monetary sense, the dead corpse of something that once had energy and commitment to something or other, but is now a resource, occasionally, for graphic design or accumulative art history courses.

I delivered something akin to these lines on the industrial picket line at University College London at the end of 2019 – for there was a strike, again, in the university sector and the default mode of doing a strike now in the UK is to have classes on the picket line, the line of striking union members who stand in front of a building and try to persuade others not to cross the line, not to work, or to study, there on that day, when labour has been withdrawn by many and solidarity is required. In the past years, these picket lines have included 'teach outs,' a kind of strike as 'happening,' performative, disruptive, an educational experience barked through a megaphone like agit-prop. I had spoken on the picket line before, in 2014, alongside Sean Bonney, who read poems while others denounced the latest government policies that undermined the accessibility of the university and worsened the conditions of its workforce. In 2014, I spoke of Walter Benjamin's passionate words about youth and experience and how experience is used as a stick with which to beat young people who lack it.[1] I was motivated to address the picket line again, in 2019, with Paul Gilroy and Matthew Beaumont, to talk through an indistinct megaphone to students who may or may not have crossed it. Sean Bonney had just committed suicide in Berlin, aged 50. Here is an extract of one of his poems:

> Please don't cry. Time will come.
> Bear that in mind. Remember.
> Don't look at me. Don't cry.
> We are gathering the pieces.
> There will be no locked doors.
> No officials, no murders, no slaves.
> Sometimes we'll speak in colours,
> in musical notes. No passwords,
> no secret codes. But remember,
> serious, keep a pill in your mouth.
> Keep it there, these words there:
> solitude, profit, humiliation, suicide.
> That's the dictionary of history.
> When they shoot it at us, fire back.
> I can't lie. Things will get harder,
> but keep at it. Despite our violence
> our addictions. All this burning earth.[2]

The poem calls on a certain collective. Our violence. Our addictions. We are gathering the pieces. But we also hold on to the means of our own death, should it all go wrong. And it goes wrong. This vision is a fight against a hostile environment and we act collectively and we go down as one body in

---

1   Walter Benjamin, "Experience" [1913], *Walter Benjamin: Selected Writings, 1: 1913–1926*, (Cambridge, MA: Harvard University Press, 2004), 3-5.

2   Sean Bonney, *All This Burning Earth: Selected Writings of Sean Bonney* (New York: Ill Will Editions, 2016), 60.

unity or broken into pieces, taking solace from our common misery. Where is my collective? And what manifesto might today's collectives write – collectives that were not formed like the first ones in the now impossibly opulent and Romantic sounding surroundings, in the dead of night, 'beneath mosque lamps whose brass cupolas are bright as our souls' and 'trampling underfoot our native sloth on opulent Persian carpets.'[3] For the most part, a contemporary collective would at least not admit such wealthy environs, would at least present itself comprised of those who are of the people, a Here Comes Everybody, in the manner of Joyce's universal any-man character of *Finnegans Wake*, HCE. Or even, and perhaps more likely, a collective today would underscore its parts as composed of those who are cast out, precarious, on the edge of things, power, and wealth. Things will get harder, but keep at it. Things get harder for those who feel themselves addressed by the poem. To be on the edge is hard. To be avant-garde is hard – harder still even than it was, because there is no place for it, not even an uncomfortable one. And even if individual good fortune occurs, our social body is hurting.

The first manifesto of the modern epoch – the one that conjures into being a conception of capitalism as a world force – is the Communist one by Marx and Engels, from 1848, and it commences with ghosts haunting Europe. I too, like many of us, spent the last years communing with other ghosts – with the dead people who have written some of the books, as well as pixel ghosts on Zoom channels that are the grave of being. I thought some of the thoughts that follow – or ones close to them – in the days after I heard Sean Bonney had died. They came, then, through a ghost, an afterlife, the end of a life, which had been in many ways a rear-guard, holding operation on the avant-garde.

---

3   Quotations from the opening lines of *The Futurist Manifesto* (1909).

I went, in 2019, on the picket line, trying to bring into proximity the poetic and the political, in my own emulation of avant-garde procedures, to say something like this:

Sean Bonney was an anarchist, or an anarcho-communist – uncomfortable in some ways with Trade Union politics, with which we are now engaged. He was more comfortable in the squatted occupations, such as the student occupations of 2010, which were a large and loud movement in opposition to spending cuts in education and increased student fees – and whose demonstrations felt the full force of the police baton on several occasions. Within this movement, he met a younger generation of political, aesthetical comrades, who have recently mourned his departure, deeply. Those 2010 occupations were passionate, wild affairs where the being-different, being-collective of all life was evoked. There, the promises of a liberated life, and a closeness of art and life, of bringing art into life and life into art, amid the usual politicking and the all too usual outrages of abuse that occur even in radical scenes, were trialled. The university in reinvention absorbs the wishes of a revolutionary avant-garde. The students and their comrades protested against prosaic things – the planned spending cuts to further education and an increase of the cap on tuition fees by the Conservative-Liberal Democrat coalition government. But they also germinated a new vocabulary of social centres, including one close to the UCL picket line – within sight, across the square. At this one, the Bloomsbury Social Centre, Bonney was just one of many who visited, spoke, agitated, read poems, created. To protest against the university, to argue specifically in 2010, as in 2014, 2018, 2019, for in all these years there was widespread agitation against the university as it exists, is to propose a new university, or more, to enact it – to set up through the processes of taking control of a situation provides the possibility of taking control of the whole situation and learning and unlearning together. And extending learning and knowing beyond the disciplinary structures of the university. In 2010, Bonney joined the occupation in Gordon Square in London, one of a thousand activities where the students cultivated links to other university members, the cleaners, for one. The students lost in 2010. But the occupations left their mark on those who went into them and came through them. After this movement of 2010, Bonney left London to become a research fellow in Berlin at the John F. Kennedy's Literature Department, studying the work of Beat poet, Diane di Prima. That produced discomfort, in some ways, though the stability of a salary must have been useful, gratifying.

We are gathering the pieces. He gathered the pieces – continued to gather them in Europe. Bonney gathered the pieces of a fragmented and exhausted avant-garde. Working backwards, in time, one can see his engagements – folded into poetry and critical writings and academic work – with British punk, the Angry Brigade, Baader-Meinhof and the Rote Armee Fraktion, Black Panthers and Black Power, especially Leroi Jones/Amiri Baraka. But there was a wellspring, for he was drawn to the origins of the avant-garde in revolutionary France, to the culture of Paris Commune France, the conspiracies of Baudelaire, the horror visions of Blanqui, the delirium of Rimbaud and Verlaine. Sometimes we'll speak in colours, in musical notes, like Rimbaud. Rather than striking, the workaday limited withdrawal of labour in the quest for something as reformist as better pay and conditions, he might have been more attracted to Paul Lafargue's tract from the 1880s: *Le Droit à la paresse*. The Right to be Lazy or the Right to Idleness. Lafargue was responding to and parodying the socialist demand for a right to work. To not do or do nothing. Negation. Not doing, A resistance. It is not laziness re-evaluated as a positive trait or a resistant act, but a not doing. An Undoing or to undo doing. It proposed the demand to think the unthinkable, undo the doing, do the undoing. Not wanting to work or go to work, or do work. Work is the problem – poets work while dreaming, or some of them think they do.

During the lecturer strikes of 2019 and 2020, I was struck by the outpouring of misery, of exhaustion, of anger that coursed through social media. Lecturers testified to 100-hour weeks, to 3 hours sleep each night, to vicious managers, to abuse in the workplace, to an impossibility to keep up, to a future immiseration, to a desire to leave or never begin in this field of employment, once so desirable, even if always demanding something deep from the self, as a thing of passion, a confusion of self and job. Sometimes perhaps, in these status updates, that, like any status, were paraded to outdo the others, I detected hyperbole. This is a poetic technique of using exaggeration to produce strong effect. In "Defence of Poetry," Percy Bysshe Shelley states that poets are the unacknowledged legislators of the world. In being poetic, they, we, feel the world, absorb it and vomit it out again and, in picking through the causes of our sickness, we know it better than our daytime selves, or management deepfake bot-selves. Sean Bonney's poetry was hyperbolic – taking seriously that line in Adorno's *Minima Moralia*: "Knowledge comes to us through a network of prejudices, opinions, innervations, self-corrections, presuppositions and exaggerations, in short through the dense, firmly-grounded and by no means uniformly transparent medium of experience."[4] And how far do we push it? We push it as far as we need to in order to glimpse something other. Only exaggerations are true in the field of knowledge of the self and revolutionising the world – to adapt, again, Adorno's phrase in *Minima Moralia*: "In psycho-analysis nothing is true except the exaggerations."[5] It is at the limits of sense that the nonsense we exist within is unmasked. Only when it is pushed beyond the plausible, can the truth to the lie appear. It is worse than we can even say, because its horror exceeds our capacity to contain it in the language of regular discourse. But

---

4   Theodor W. Adorno, *Minima Moralia* [1951] (London: Verso, 2006), 80.

5   Ibid., 49.

remember, serious, keep a pill in your mouth. Keep it there, these words there: solitude, profit, humiliation, suicide. That's the dictionary of history.

Sean Bonney was wont to cite a line from Jean Genet, in "Letter to the American Intellectuals," a talk given at the University of Connecticut, on 18 March 1970. First published as "Bobby Seale, the Black Panthers and Us White People," in *Black Panther Newspaper*, on 28 March 1970, it averred the proximity of poetry and revolution: "As for the political thought of the Black Panthers, I am convinced it originates in the poetic thought of Black Americans.

We are realizing more and more that a poetic emotion lies at the origin of revolutionary thought."[6]

The words are good advice for turning the pain of being into a pain against being, a poetics of refusal. Genet's line about the proximity of political theory and poetic practice, then wanders into a territory that Bonney does not enter. Genet writes: "This is why we have to understand that it is on the basis of singular poetic emotions that Mao Tse-Tung was led to revolutionary consciousness, later on to the Long March, then to the revolution called the 'Hundred Flowers' campaign, and, finally, to the Cultural Revolution. And it was the same for Ho Chi Minh.

And the same is true for the Black Panther Party, which from the poetic resources of their oppressed people draws the will to elaborate a rigorous revolutionary thought."[7]

---

6   Cited in Sean Bonney, "Notes on Militant Poetics 3/3," https://poetry.openlibhums.org/article/id/9255

7   Jean Genet, "Letter to American Intellectuals" [1970], *The Declared Enemy: Texts and Interviews* (Stanford: Stanford University Press, 2004), 32.

Genet never stopped being a self-proclaimed 'vagabond' in order to become a revolutionary.[8] Genet did not wield poetry to underline all that is good, beautiful, and pure – rather it was in its 'cursedness and their negativity, which disclose, according to Genet, the possibility for an "entirely different human adventure".'[9] A Hero, in Bonney's pantheon, along with Situationist Mustapha Khayati, Dante, Rimbaud, and Baudelaire. Genet is revered by Bonney for his vagabondage, rebuttals, and shamelessness: "But his hatred for your world would be the same. His fist, his knife, his negligee."[10] Genet succumbed, at least in rhetoric, to the Maoist illusion that suffused the Black Panthers, and he could not extricate himself from his time, from the pressures of his time to ally with what appeared as its most progressive forces. Some student activists went in that direction – thinking this was vanguardism. Genet could not isolate himself from its movements flowing through him, from the thinking that is done for him and in him. Genet campaigned for anti-imperialism at home and abroad – he used the university system to appeal to white students to gain support for the Black Panthers. He used the fringes of that system – not the system itself, which is for the most part and usually and still against knowledge, because it is for disciplinary specialisms and the rewarding of conventional thinking, of thinking within convention and for convention. Something different happens when learning takes place outside of this – not competitively but collectively and in close accord with

---

8   Cited in Jean Genet, "May Day Speech," *The Declared Enemy: Texts and Interviews*, 34. For a thorough exploration of Genet's involvement with the Black Panthers, see Jackqueline Frost, "Jean Genet's May Day Speech, 1970: 'Your Real Life Depends on the Black Panther Party'," *Social Text Online*, 1 May 2020, here: https://socialtextjournal.org/jean-genets-may-day-speech-1970-your-real-life-depends-on-the-black-panther-party

9   As quoted in Frost, ibid.

10   See Bonney, http://abandonedbuildings.blogspot.com/2019/09/?m=1

the grain of life and love. This is the poetry of which Genet speaks – emotions leading to consciousness; words transforming ideas transforming actions. That he was consumed by what was happening on the world stage – the rise of Maoism in Europe, the partiality for Ho Chi Minh as an act of anti-imperialist commitment – cannot be subtracted from what it means to rethink the world as the world rethinks itself. And in thought mingles much that is dead, or wrong, but thought is living and breathing and so can make mistakes. Is that process of meddling and meshing in the world a form of 'thinking for and in itself,' or is it something else – the world becoming conscious of itself, of how thought, theory, ideas steer, like a sail, the winds of history, the wounds of history?

Thinking happens in a place, in a time. I read Lukács' "Antinomies of Bourgeois Thought" first when I was in an occupation at the University of Sussex in the 1980s. It was my homework reading for a class with Gillian Rose. To read it there, in the occupied administrative building of the University of Sussex, with the pressures of that moment, that space, outside the seminar room, while being simultaneously threatened with expulsion from the university and the invasion of the police, meant that it came to make sense, as a self-critical enactment of what praxis is. In that setting, the "The Antimonies of Bourgeois Thought" came to make crystalline sense.[11] Is the space of avant-garde thought para-academic then, dependent on but rejecting the academic mode, because that appears to be the mode where thought towards change is sanctioned? More commonly thought is subjected to reifying pressures, observes Lukács. Reification produces a contemplative stance vis-à-vis the world. This can be sceptical, pragmatic, practical,

---

11   See Georg Lukács, *History and Class Consciousness: Studies in Marxist Dialectics* [1923] (Cambridge, MA: MIT Press, 1971), esp. "The Antinomies of Bourgeois Thought," 110-48.

submissive in the face of an unchangeable world of quantities with which, and in which, we have simply to live. Or it is antithetical to itself: our introspection leads to dreaming, to an ethical demand, to Romantic thoughts and utopian ideals. A residual sense persists within our being that we are more than quantity, that we are imaginative humans with wandering, errant thoughts, even poetic ones. But the contemplative stance remains helpless, imprisoned in thought and only thought, infused by world, which oppresses it, but not infusing it. This occurs because the object of the contemplative stance, the reified self, is cast into the position only of reacting and not acting, and in any case, Lukács notes, such contemplation may be nonetheless demanding of time and demoralizing of spirit to those compelled by it. To watch empty, purely quantitative time pass without being able to dive into it and affect it is to contemplate the world as something that happens to the self, not a communal cosmos to be remade. Reification cannot be overcome in thought, in or for itself – but it might be pulled apart and assailed in poetry. And through that something is re-fused, and there is a glimpse at freedom, of other-thinking.

And the dictionary of history gives us, wannabe avant-gardists of the twenty-first century, a set of poses, some attitudes, some garb to dress up in – like Rimbaud, like Baudelaire, like Amiri Baraka, like a Paris Communard, like a Black Panther – for it is as if, in the bleakest moments, we might think that the avant-garde might only be cosplayed today, in a world in which there is little hope in the combustible potential of art and politics, and only the recognition of the wounding nature of the split between them, made all the more visible in being traversed. And into the gap between them that finds no way of being healed, the avant-garde poet falls, fatally. But it is not cosplay. It is an eternal, but historically contingent necessity. Political revolution will conspire with artistic revolution – and it may wear the clothes of the past or it might rip them to pieces, but be unable to shed them. The precedents were too powerful. In his 1936 Marxist analysis, *The Marketplace of Art*, Czech avant-gardist Karel Teige characterises three types of Romanticisms formed in the wake of clerical restoration and the protectionism of the July Monarchy. There is the Conservative and reactionary Romanticism of Chateaubriand, the liberal Romanticism of Victor Hugo and Delacroix, and there is "the Dark Romanticism, the Romanticism of revolt and revolution, the aggressive and rebellious 'genre maudit' at whose inception stood authors that Georg Brandes, in his *Main Currents in Nineteenth-Century Literature*, placed in his chapter "the Overlooked and Forgotten," – poets who were later called 'poètes maudits'; this third, revolutionary current of Romanticism became the destiny of all new poetry, establishing a pedigree stretching from Borel to Breton, from Daumier to Max Ernst."[12]

The pedigree is also an anti-pedigree – the bloodline does not thrive, but withers in hostile worlds. But it remains the destiny, or destination of all new poetry, even that of the avant-garde after the avant-garde, after the multi-pronged recuperation, both of politics and art. Perhaps the possibilities contained in a philosophy of freedom, one forwarded after almost enthusiastically by the bourgeoise, have been stymied too often. Attention turns, in an age of the self, to the capacities of the broken self, the nihilistic energies of being shattered. What of our fragments, our partial glimpses, reflect a pool of possibility – the leap into freedom? Poetry becomes the conscious assertion of subjectivity as it registers both the pain of the world and its possible supersession: wound and word and world. Maybe. Poetry is a whiff of the future that should come to be, not the one we will likely get. Poetry is a bomb of words. Poetry is the barrel of a righteous gun. Poetry is not that thing you think it

---

12   Karel Teige, *The Marketplace of Art, vol. 1* [1936] (Helsinki: Rab-Rab Press, 2022), 55.

is – to do with flowers and the lyric I – it is a scarring in and of language that has registered hurt but still says no. It is a line delivered as negation of the prosaic. It is a manifesto. It is a marking of the line that should not be crossed. As is the picket line. The picket line is a small stab at future thinking, at other-being. Bonney brings the picket line – small revolution – together with poetic form, and with the cosmos or planetary, the space of collective dreaming, in "Cell 1 / Suite 3 / as in Crisis," Friday October 26, 2012:

> ok think this / or as in scabies, social ones
> in any fiscal exit, in any skaldic bullet glass
> is spinning: like the scorn of andromeda
> would compress our picket cells, as infinite
> scratch that / with all your social nails, like
> literally, inside our cutting waters, nails, like
> inside our stuttered fall / & capital is mind
> o frozen predicate: as in any social microbe
> is mundane and berserk, as any slave ship, as
> any social drunken boat, as in any scabrous
> general strike, o scarab: would scratch this
> numbered surface bone / like our finite scorn
> of prison nails / this thing has fourteen lines
> as in picket lines / like venus in a closing sky[13]

This thing – this poem – like a picket line – is composed of lines and these lines will block all too comprehensible meaning, as they will block those who would too easily parse them or traverse them. These lines, this picket line, will be in this version also redolent of love – because without passion what point political action? Venus, love goddess, will shine all the more brightly as protest in a closing horizon of possibility. This thing with fourteen lines is reified. It is a thing. It is only a thing, but

---

13   http://abandonedbuildings.blogspot.com/2012

it is also the absorbent pad of our pains and the thing that can stand as a bulwark against everything going on just as it is. This thing is possibly beyond us and everything, but it also contains us. This thing is a sonnet, but if that speaks of formal elements and being trapped by a structure that weighs on the poem like a nightmare on the brains of the living, this thing, or sonnet, can be made militant. It can speak of picket lines and evoke the lyricism gone sour in a world gone rotten of a previous epoch (such as Rimbaud's drunken boat that is made to recognise the existence on the same seas of slave ships) – just as Brecht did too, in his vulgarisations of Dante.[14]

Bonney cites the French revolutionary Blanqui as a fold in to a poem titled "Lamenation," in his collection *All This Burning Earth*, as well as on his blog *Abandoned Buildings: Monsters of the Market*, which remains a continuing ghost presence on the internet. "It is the stupid practice of our times to complain instead of acting. Jeremiads are the fashion. Jeremiah is found in all attitudes. He cries, he lashes, he dogmatises, he dictates, he rages, himself the scourge of all scourges. Let us leave the elegising clowns, those gravediggers of liberty. The duty of a revolutionary is to always struggle, to struggle no matter what, to struggle to extinction."[15]

So we are to struggle on, as we become extinct, in ever fainter after echoes of previous vanguardism practice, whose proof of radicalism is probably their failure. If they did not fail, they would not have been worth the light – or they would have made themselves too available for what exists already. We have one duty – to go beyond denunciation into action on the world,

---

14   For a reflection on this, see Jochen Vogt, "Unlikely Company: Brecht and Dante," Helen Fehervary and Bernd Fischer (eds.), *Kulturpolitik und Politik der Kultur/ Cultural Politics and the Politics of Culture* (Oxford: Peter Lang, 2007), 457-72.

15   Sean Bonney, *All This Burning Earth: Selected Writings of Sean Bonney*, 65.

destructive, transformative, provocative. But the world might not reciprocate that action. We go down fighting. Blanqui ended up defeated one too many times. He is trapped in a prison of the world, the world to come, that is far worse than that of the Bastille, for it is illimitable and will be projected by him into the outer reaches of the cosmos, eternity by the stars.[16] Yet he will continue to struggle, scream against the whole world and all that is wrong within it, whose wrongness only replicates more wrong, more and greater wrongness. We are forever outmanoeuvred by what exists and oppresses us in ever new ways. Bonney's poetic response to Blanqui locates what bears down on us, makes us despair and hope in a circular repetitive motion – the lines following the epigraph by Blanqui: "laws to scratch your childhood," "cells," "gods stashed below your bed," "fairy tales their blue love" and Bonney comments, poetically, but as an admonition, or as a manifesto demand:

> remember it
> to take these tales
> as advice
> an organising vortex
> each sentence stolen
> each word a double claw. Act now.

Words as claws, double claws, redoubled claws, books as weapons, purloined form the canons that threaten to force them into conformism – all that. Traditions handed down as that which will destroy tradition, the broken fragments of wisdom to be recycled to finally make the passage from air to act.

We do not know what new things we will be compelled to disagree with, but we know they will arrive. And we, this avantgarde inspired radical collective, have our principles: we set

---

16   Louis-Auguste Blanqui, *Eternity by the Stars: an astronomical hypothesis* [1872] (New York: Contra Mundum Press, 2013).

ourselves against instrumentalisation, against utilitarianism, against knowledge as profit-generation, against poetry as culture industry or advertising. We might be for the socialisation of our thinking or the collectivisation of our thinking. When poetry is declaimed on the picket line at the university a proposal is made to think the university universally, which might mean to unthink it – and to both smash, replace and leave behind the 'natural,' irrational and actually existing bonds of the academy, in a move towards freedom, while tying ourselves up in new institutions that can only tend towards the ossification of thinking if it is not in constant argument with itself, recovering poetic reserves of injustice and intuition within itself. Slipping and sliding to not allow that which we have made but has become objective rule over us. To escape our time, our place, our language, while being so thoroughly trapped by it, pushing outwards, sucking in, being a collective subject on the point of discovering its potential agency, countering mood with wish, smashing language and sense into poetry, rejecting poetry in favour of riot, insisting on the identity of those two things, however absurdly, and setting language and action wildly into the world in whatever way we can.

Of course, poetry in the service of struggle has its limits. Bonney's *Further Notes on Militant Poetics* casts doubt on any space of liberation proposed by poetry as immune to the abuses of power. Everything can be recuperated by business. Capital too has a poetics or rather an anti-poetics more determined than that of anti-art – its poetics comes as force, a direct communication against the body, flexed by an entity – the corporate body – that lashes out in its own image, desensitizing, denying. Bonney challenges the continuing veracity of Aimé Césaire's proposition from the 1940s – "poetic knowledge is born in the great silence of scientific knowledge"[17]. It is no longer the case that these knowledges are counterposed, claims Bonney. Instead, "both have been sucked into the non-cognitive counter-vortex of corporate knowledge, in which there are no senses to derange, in which all is, as Marx put it, 'devoid of eyes, of teeth, of ears, of everything.'[18] There is only corporate knowledge – a science of corporations, HR, business studies, market prediction and so on, and capital. Bonney will state, has its own poetics. The poetics that an avant-gardist or critical figure might conjure as hex against the corporates possesses an 'absolute irrelevance to corporate nihilism.'[19] It cannot be of use to business. But that does not, he claims, make it the opposite of money. "And it is certainly not, as the fatuous Franco Beradi would claim, revolutionary on account of being a somehow authentic, unmediated communication, as if anything could be. There is, in any case, no more 'authentic' communication than the corporate state's power to refuse you food, shelter and life. Workfare and zero-hours contracts are the poetics of capital. Poetic knowledge, alongside scientific, philosophical, historic, political, militant knowledge are collectively the great silence, the great defect and instability at the centre of corporate knowledge. By virtue of that collectivity, and only though it, they still have their chance."[20]

Poetic knowledge, if it is militant knowledge, or critical knowledge, and so worthy of the name of avant-garde, has no accord with corporate knowledge and its poetics of denial and wage

---

17   Quotation of Cesaire from "Poetry and Knowledge" [1944], *Refusal of the Shadow: Surrealism and the Caribbean* (London: Verso, 1996), 134.

18   Bonney, *All This Burning Earth*, 27.

19   Ibid., 45.

20   http://abandonedbuildings.blogspot.com/2013/09/further-notes-on-militant-poetics.html

labour – nor with the skills based, employer-needs agenda now coshing UK academia.[21] Who has the revolutionary daring still which flings at the adversary the defiant words: "I am nothing but I must be everything."[22] Bonney's is a thermal dialectic – we are made nothing, no senses, no autonomy, trapped in zero hours contracts, as is the technique of labour contracts in UK neo-liberalism. We are nothing – but we might still want to be everything. This burning earth, this earth will burn and might at least in the process warm us up as we huddle collectively in refusal, including the refusal of the avant-garde to die.

---

21   For just one example of this, see speech by Minister Halfon, Minister for Skills, Apprenticeships and Higher Education, 16 November 2022: https://www.gov.uk/government/speeches/minister-halfon-speech-at-the-times-higher-education-conference.

22   Karl Marx and Friedrich Engels, "A Contribution to the Critique of Hegel's Philosophy of Right" [1843], *On Religion* (New York: Dover Publications, 2008), 55.

From Art Strike to the Abolition of Art: Breton, Jouffroy, and the Murder of Art

Abigail Susik

One of the earliest proposals for the concept of an "art strike" is also one of the most overlooked examples of this tactic and theory in scholarship. In mid-January of 1925, the surrealist author André Breton published an editorial, "La Dernière grève" [The Last Strike] in the opening pages of the second issue of the new Parisian journal he helped produce, *La Révolution surréaliste* [Surrealist revolution]. Breton's essay discusses the tentative economic value of cultural and intellectual production in capitalist economy and calls for artists, philosophers, and scholars to undertake a general strike for a period lasting between several nights to one year.[1] The production of all artworks, theory, and research would cease entirely for the duration of the strike period. The goal of Breton's final strike or ultimate stand is for creative producers and knowledge workers, as we might call them in today's parlance, to align in solidarity with blue-collar labour in a parallel struggle to win fair conditions and wages.

Although the surrealists and their compatriots never undertook such a protest, Breton's mid-1920s proposal stands as one of the boldest statements of the art strike concept ever articulated. The Bretonian art strike becomes all the more significant when it is comprehended in conjunction with the

---

1   André Breton, "La Dernière grève," *La Révolution surréaliste* 2, 1925, 1-3.

overarching surrealist "war on work" and the surrealist ethos of permanent strike, which amounted to an attempted, if not always successful or consistent, group praxis of lifelong resistance to the wage labour imperative under capitalism.[2] Influenced by the legacy of anarchism in France, including local histories of sabotage and strike, Breton's essay advocates for direct action through the mutual alignment of independent intellectuals and artists, rather than through the formation of a union or adhesion to a particular political party.[3]

Moreover, Breton's "Last Strike" essay influenced another and much more well-known call for an art strike by a French writer who was closely aligned with surrealism, Alain Jouffroy. In the growing scholarly literature on art strikes, Jouffroy's brief summons to an "active art strike" in his 1968 essay, "What's To Be Done About Art? From the Abolition of Art to Revolutionary Individualism," has been frequently as the one of the first expressions of this idea, along with art strike statements, art boycott actions, or principled withdrawals from and stoppages of art production by the Situationist International, the

---

2   Abigail Susik, *Surrealist Sabotage and the War on Work* (Manchester: Manchester University Press, 2021).

3   During the 1930s, however, Breton was involved with artist unions: the AEAR (Association of Revolutionary Artists and Writers), organized in collaboration with André Thirion and others in 1930; and the Fédération internationale de l'art révolutionnaire indépendant (FIARI), formed in Mexico with Trotsky in 1938. For an overview of the history of direct action and theoretical art strikes, see Stewart Martin, "Art Strikes: An Inventory," *Mute* (May 1, 2020), n.p. https://www.metamute.org/editorial/articles/art-strikes-inventory. Martin does not mention Breton's 1925 "Last Strike" essay but clarifies that Jouffroy was not the first person to cultivate the art strike concept. Also see Stevphen Shukaitis, "Art Strikes and The Metropolitan Factory," *A Joy Forever: The Political Economy of Social Creativity* (London: MayFly Books, 2011), 227–236; Stevphen Shukaitis, *The Composition of Movements to Come: Aesthetics and Cultural Labour After the Avant-Garde* (London: Rowman & Littlefield, 2016), 71–75, 94–97.

Art Workers' Coalition, Lee Lozano, Gustav Metzger, Stewart Home, and other individuals and groups between the 1950s and the 1990s.[4] As such, Jouffroy's essay, written in the context of the upheavals in France during May 1968, has become a touchstone for contemporary iterations of the art strike concept in the last three decades. Yet, aside from the dubious (and, in this case, erroneous) practice of naming originary "firsts" in the construction of historical teleologies, important nuances of Jouffroy's essay are lost when the profound influence of Bretonian surrealism, and indeed, the broader context of surrealism itself, are obscured in the discourse. Jouffroy's call for an art strike is best understood as an echo and expansion of Breton's radical proposal a generation prior.

The purpose of this essay is to analyse Breton's 1925 "Last Strike" essay in relation to Jouffroy's late-1960s statements on the art strike and the revolutionary abolition of art, in order to determine the differences and similarities between their approaches, and to demonstrate how surrealism is essential to Jouffroy's theories. Why has Breton's editorial been ignored

---

4   Alain Jouffroy, "What's To Be Done About Art? From the Abolition of Art to Revolutionary Individualism" [1968], *Art and Confrontation: France and the Arts in an Age of Change* (London: Studio Vista, 1970), 181; emphasis original. For texts that name Jouffroy as the earliest or first progenitor of the art strike concept, see, for example: Jacopo de Blasio, "About the Strike of Art," *Juliet* (June 29, 2020). https://www.juliet-artmagazine.com/en/about-the-strike-of-art/. Stewart Home, "About the Art Strike," *The Art Strike Papers*, eds. Stewart Home and James Mannox (Stirling: AK Press, 1991), 1. Other relevant texts include: Jo Applin, *Lee Lozano: Not Working* (New Haven: Yale University Press, 2018). Julia Bryan-Wilson, *Art Workers: Radical Practice in the Vietnam War Era* (Berkeley: University of California Press, 2009). For discussions of contemporary art strikes in the new millennium, see, for example: Joanna Warsza, ed. *I Can't Work Like This: a Reader on Recent Boycotts and Contemporary Art* (Berlin: Sternberg Press, 2017). Kuba Szreder, "Productive Withdrawals: Art Strikes, Art Worlds, and Art as a Practice of Freedom." *e-flux Journal*, no. 87 (2017), https://www.e-flux.com/journal/87/168899/productive-withdrawals-art-strikes-art-worlds-and-art-as-a-practice-of-freedom/.

heretofore in the literature on art strikes, especially considering the prominence of Jouffroy's later proposition of an "active art strike" in the formation of a genealogy for this concept, as well as the clear ties of Jouffroy's life and work to surrealism? Although scholars in the field of surrealism studies have frequently discussed and cited Breton's 1925 essay in scholarship devoted to the surrealist movement, this abundance of citations has not had an apparent impact on non-specialists interested in the art strike concept.[5] Such a trend could be the result of practical issues, such as the fact that Breton's essay, nearly a century old, is short and remains untranslated into English, or it could be couched in other reasons related to the often-biased reception of surrealism in various texts and disciplines over the last century.[6]

I argue that Breton's art strike statement has been occluded in part due to some of the ideological premises of his essay relating to the separation between the proletariat and intellectuals, and because of Jouffroy's later assertions that an art strike is just one preliminary step towards the realized revolutionary condition of a world in which the concept of art itself is entirely

---

5   See, for example, among other sources that discuss Breton's 1925 art strike proposal: Alastair Hemmens, *The Critique of Work in Modern French Thought: From Charles Fourier to Guy Debord* (New York: Palgrave Macmillan, 2019), 121–22. Theresa Papanikolas, *Anarchism and the Advent of Paris Dada: Art and Criticism, 1914–1924* (Burlington, VT: Ashgate, 2009), 159. Richard David Sonn, *Sex, Violence, and the Avant-garde: Anarchism in Interwar France* (University Park: Pennsylvania State University Press, 2010), 80–82.

6   In one obvious example of such bias in the context of the literature on art strikes, Stewart Home, a proponent of art strike, describes surrealism as, "the most degenerate expression of the Utopian tradition." Stewart Home, *The Assault on Culture: Utopian Currents from Lettrisme to Class War* (London: AK Press, 1991), 5. In his 1965 lecture "Auto-Destructive Art," Gustav Metzger argued that the roots of auto-destructive art were in dada, but he does not mention surrealism. Gustav Metzger, "Auto-destructive Art" (1965), *Gustav Metzger: Damaged Nature, Auto-Destructive Art* (London: Coracle@workfortheeyetodo, 1997), 25.

abolished. If in 1925, Breton's notion of artistic and intellectual work as a manifestly exploited type of labour bore the connotations of radical solidarity across classes in support of a coming revolution in both base and superstructure, by 1968 Jouffroy's surrealist foundations had become outmoded in the face of the revolution unfolding in the present – those of *Mai '68*. It is important to realize that while Jouffroy does mention art strike as a placeholder tactic, his primary interest in "What's To Be Done About Art?" is his forecast of the approaching Death of Art in a post-capitalist society. Since art, as such, is a reflection of the capitalist economy for Jouffroy, given its typical commodity or luxury commodity status, the notion of "art" must be obliterated in a future revolutionary society.

In this regard, art strike histories in general can benefit from a broader contextual understanding of the Bretonian art strike concept generated in the immediate post-World War I period. Jouffroy's articulation dramatically pushed beyond that concept, rather than simply reiterating it; but the latter idea remains solidly couched in the former. Conceptualizing art strikes in relation to theories of the abolition of art can likewise offer dynamic theoretical perspectives on the immediate goals of contemporary practices like Metzger's auto-destructive practices within the capitalist system. If an art strike is envisioned as a temporary stoppage or cessation of production in protest against exploitation, and a preliminary stage in the formulation of demands on the workers' terms, then it remains a resistance tactic ultimately rooted in acceptance of the capitalism. Art strike is a tool used for reform. The abolition of the category of art altogether, in contrast, presumes the obsolescence of capitalism and the creation of altogether new socio-cultural relations.

Breton's "La Dernière grève" (1925)

André Breton's proposal for a strike of artists and intellectuals in January of 1925 coincided with the birth of surrealism in the autumn and winter of 1924–25, including the publication of Breton's *Manifesto of Surrealism* and the initial issues of the journal *Surrealist Revolution*, as well as the establishment of the Bureau of Surrealist Research in Paris. "The Last Strike," which clearly states Breton's steadfast anarchist sympathies at the time, was also written a few months in advance of Breton's revived interest in the French Communist Party (PCF). Breton had attempted to join the newly formed PCF in the winter of 1920 but was ultimately discouraged by the extensive level of bureaucracy required of new adherents.[7] It was not until the summer of 1925 that Breton and other surrealists began to collaborate with socialist publications and members of the PCF on anti-colonial protests in opposition to the entry of France into the Spanish-led Moroccan Rif War. Likewise, the surrealists did not proclaim their "war on work" until the July 1925 issue of *La Révolution surréaliste*, number four, was published. Breton's editorial, "The Last Strike," from January of that year, is thus an essay that manifests Breton's consciousness of the possible contribution of the intelligentsia to leftist struggles like the French labour movement and the critique of wage labour, but it is not a statement of political affiliation. There is no explicit link, for instance, between Breton's essay and Soviet director Sergei Eisenstein's silent film drama *Strike*, which was released a few months later, in April of 1925. In all likelihood, Breton's interest in the protest tactic of the strike was primarily inspired by the attention he had paid to French anarchist activities since his teenage years, in advance of his service in World

---

7   Mark Polizzotti, *Revolution of the Mind: The Life of André Breton* (New York: Da Capo, 1997), 149–50.

War I, as well as the wave of strikes that seized France during and immediately following the war.[8]

Although Breton's "La Dernière grève" is overarchingly a statement of solidarity with "manual" or blue-collar workers, it is one expressed in spite of what Breton claims is the impassable separation between manual workers and intellectuals. This schism between the working class and the intelligentsia is not configured by Breton as being a result of the class divide per se, although conceptualisations of class difference do arise in the scope of his discussion. Rather, from his point of view, it is a result of divergent shortcomings on both sides of the equation that render the artist and the worker disparate from one another, as well as the incommensurate misery of manual workers as compared to intellectuals. For Breton, it is the proletariat who will drive the revolution against capitalism, not painters and poets, who would do their best to step aside and stay out of the way.

Breton commences his remarks by critiquing the faithful work ethic of the masses on the factory floor. Rather than instigating total revolt against the system of wage labour, Breton opines, modern workers retain pride in their work and merely negotiate for temporary alleviations of their woes in successive struggles for reforms. They "affirm their right to live on the very

---

8   Papanikolas, *Anarchism and the Advent of Paris Dada,* in passim. It is not likely that in this era Breton had already read *Réflexions sur la violence* (1908) by the revolutionary syndicalist theorist Georges Sorel. Sorel theorized the general strike (*grève générale*) as the mythic force that would unite the working class in the destruction of bourgeois culture. Georges Sorel, *Reflections on Violence* (1908; New York: Cambridge University Press, 1999). In a 1921 essay Walter Benjamin weighs the question of the inherent violence of the strike as a form of extortion and non-action and follows Sorel in his praise for the divine and law-destroying violence of the proletarian general strike. Breton would not have had access to Benjamin's response to Sorel. See Walter Benjamin, "Critique of Violence," *Reflections: Essays, Aphorisms, Autobiographical Writing* (New York: Schocken Books, 1986), 277–300.

principle of their slavery," Breton insists, and they "cultivate the notion of work in a quasi-religious way."[9] This widespread attitude about the "sacred character of work" is considered an egregious prejudice by Breton because it hinders the full range of oppositional thought and action. Therefore, even while Breton calls for artists and intellectuals to join workers in the fierce labour struggles that characterized the first half of the 1920s, especially in France, he also underscores the profound rift [la scission] that separates manual workers from knowledge and cultural workers.[10] He admits from the outset, therefore, that an art strike is fundamentally distinct from other types of strike actions, and he proceeds to expose some of the key contradictions inherent in this concept of a work stoppage enacted by the intelligentsia.

First, Breton claims that workers have a right to resent intellectuals because the full force of blue-collar "anger" has so often been diverted away from its revolutionary impetus through the interventions of learned pundits who would speak for them, dulling the violence of labour's fury.[11] Workers have been "the playthings of political mirage for too long," according to Breton, who also implies that it is in part because of the intellectual class that workers have learned to call their work sacred, thus delaying the onset of revolution.[12] "Where words have betrayed them weapons would always have been better placed," Breton states.[13] His concept of an art strike, in that case, is not only different from that of a general labour

---

9   Breton, "La Dernière grève," 1; author's translation.

10   Ibid., 1; author's translation.

11   Ibid., 1; author's translation.

12   Ibid., 1; author's translation.

13   Ibid., 1; author's translation.

strike in its means and aims. The art strike must also remain distinct from manual labour struggles so as not to continue to interfere with progress toward a revolution against capitalism in the hands of the proletariat. "We are hardly workers," Breton chides his poet comrades, pointing out the innumerable privileges that intellectuals and artists enjoy within the typical framework of independent employment, including the possibility of occupational selection and satisfaction, as well as the lack of oversight and wage control by superiors.[14]

Rather than pursuing the illusion that artwork is labour as such, which would only constitute another violation of trust from the point of view of workers, Breton asserts that the educated class must accept the limitations of their rarified position. The role of intellectuals and artists is not to instigate revolution. Instead, Breton rallies, it is their duty to "bear witness in all circumstances to our absolute attachment to the principle of human freedom" through their actions and activities, their artwork or scholarship, and by means of direct protest actions, such as art strikes.[15]

What right do artists have to strike, if they are not beset by the same woes as the proletariat – if low pay, exhaustion, and the dominance of employers are not necessarily boiling points for mass protests by intellectuals? Breton readily admits that the notion of an art strike is laughable upon first impression given the privileges enjoyed by the intelligentsia. After all, would society noticeably suffer if artists and scholars withheld their activity, he wonders? Despite this contradiction, he nonetheless affirms his confidence in the effectiveness of the art strike in terms of its amplification of the specific ilk of discontent and dissatisfaction experienced by artists and scholars *as a method of support for*

---

14   Ibid., 2; author's translation.

15   Ibid., 2; author's translation.

the workers' revolution. This is because the literati are besieged by issues of precarity, insufficient remuneration, and arbitrary hierarchies of prestige and hegemony. Since "dissatisfaction appears to be the necessary condition for a global revision of those in power" – by which he means revolution – Breton advocates for a collective protest by artists and scholars against such endemic complaints, in solidarity with the much more fundamental struggle being waged by the proletariat.[16] One of the protest demands of the art strike would be equal pay for all knowledge workers, regardless of their status and recognition. Bad poets would get paid as much as star painters. Another demand would entail the cessation of all censorship and the immediate repeal of laws persecuting and repressing "*anarchist intrigues.*"[17] Radical intellectuals would not suffer extradition or exile as a result of their seditious proclamations.

"Why not strike?," Breton queries.[18] Artists and scholars have nothing to lose, he opines, at least nothing of material importance. He indicates that an artists' trade union would not be sufficient, in his eyes, to solve the numerous problems faced by knowledge workers in post-World War I France. Likewise, he welcomes the silence that would ensue after a year without the publication of books by anyone – especially "ridiculous" books – and the nostalgia and "regret" that readers would eventually experience as they turned to outdated copies of magazines no longer produced.[19] He notes the probable effects of such a durational strike, such as the closure of bookstores and print shops due to lack of business, as well as the shocked response of university students. "Last Strike" concludes by

---

16   Ibid., 2; author's translation.

17   Ibid., 3; author's translation; emphasis original.

18   Ibid., 3; author's translation.

19   Ibid., 3; author's translation.

imagining a world without the production of new art, literature, and scholarship, implying that the art strike may be the sole means by which creative and knowledge production can be salvaged in the wreckage of capitalism. It is only through the cessation of art – at least on a temporary basis – that society will come to value art.

Jouffroy's **L'Abolition de l'art** (1967-68)

Alain Jouffroy's endorsement of the art strike occurs in the context of an essay that was published in a Belgian book during the second half of 1968 and translated into English for a British publication of the same year: "What's To Be Done About Art? From the Abolition of Art to Revolutionary Individualism."[20] Yet, hovering in the background of this essay was also a decade of leftist activism combining art and protest, such as Jouffroy's participation in staged demonstrations against the Algerian war in the early 1960s and his co-founding of a Writers' Union in the wake of the French protests in 1968.[21] His summons to a radicalized revision in the concept of art in society, "What's To Be Done...?" was written in August of 1968, just two months after the mass strikes and protests in France.

---

20   Jouffroy, "What's To Be Done About Art?," 175–201. Alain Jouffroy, "Que faire de l'art?: de l'abolition de l'art à l'individualisme révolutionnaire," *Art et contestation: Témoins et témoignages Actualité* (Bruxelles: La Connaissance, 1968), 175–202. For a recent reprint of this essay, see, Alain Jouffroy, "Que faire de l'art? De l'abolition de l'art à l'individualisme révolutionnaire," *L'Abolition de l'art* (Falaise: Impeccables, 2011).

21   Masachika Tani, "Alain Jouffroy," *The International Encyclopedia of Surrealism*, ed. Michael Richardson et al. (London: Bloomsbury, 2019), 2: 391. Also see Samuel Dudouit, *Alain Jouffroy passe sans porte* (Paris: Les Éditions du Littéraire, 2015), 201–21, 257–59.

Yet, this iconoclastic essay was equally shaped by projects that Jouffroy had been working on far in advance of *Mai '68*. Throughout the 1960s, Jouffroy was deeply invested in an art criticism discourse that featured post-dada and surrealist theories of anti-art, the Duchampian dematerialization of the artwork into the readymade, and the objecthood of visual art – particularly as manifested in contemporary art movements such as *nouveau réalisme* and Pop. In September of 1967, he wrote an essay for a catalogue entitled, *L'Abolition de l'art* [The abolition of art], published on the occasion of a February 1968 exhibition by the French artist Daniel Pommereulle at the Claude Givaudan Gallery in Paris.[22] Pommereulle's show, "Urgences" [Emergencies], featured controversial mixed-media artworks critiquing the use of torture in the Algerian War. A short film entitled *L'Abolition de l'art* (1968), narrated by Jouffroy and including footage of Pommereulle and his exhibition, was also produced by the Givaudan Gallery at this time.

Despite its title, Jouffroy's essay for Pommereulle in *L'Abolition de l'art*, provides merely a preliminary glimpse of the significantly more realized revolutionary discourse he achieved only a few months later with the follow-up essay, "What's To Be Done About Art?" The art strike tactic, for instance, is not mentioned in the Givaudan catalogue, nor is the notion of the abolition of art stated in explicitly anti-Statist and insurrectionist terms. Even so, for obvious reasons, *L'Abolition de l'art* is important to consider in the context of Jouffroy's development of the art strike and abolition of art concepts that would become so prominent in his subsequent essay, and were further elaborated in texts from the 1970s that continued to expand

---

22   Alain Jouffroy, *L'Abolition de l'art* (Genève: C. Givaudan, 1968).

on some of these themes.[23] It is also in the Givaudan catalogue that his theories about the total transformation of art in contemporary life continue to be developed in the context of his extensive ties to the French surrealist group. In particular, they are proposed in relation to his close connection to an early mentor, André Breton, who is mentioned twice in the essay alongside the names of other surrealists and surrealist associates such as Hans Bellmer, Wifredo Lam, Roberto Matta, Max Ernst, Georges Bataille, Roger Caillois, Antonin Artaud, Méret Oppenheim, Joseph Cornell, and others.[24]

Although Jouffroy was only a member of the Paris surrealist group for two years between 1946 and 1948, when he was not yet twenty years old, he considered himself to be a surrealist writer throughout his entire life.[25] After being taken under Breton's wing as a young, aspiring poet, Jouffroy never abandoned his admiration for the elder surrealist, who published some of his first poems in the surrealist journal *Néon*. The essay *L'Abolition de l'art* is an important statement of Jouffroy's continued respect for the radicalism of the surrealist movement, which, along with dada, is presented by him as being an avant-garde with revolutionary potential that was nevertheless eventually recuperated into capitalism.[26] It is "despite" dada and what he characterizes as a still-living surrealism that "all avant-garde works" gradually become mere "products of class," Jouffroy concluded in 1967.[27]

---

23   See, for instance, Alain Jouffroy, *De l'individualisme révolutionnaire* (Paris: Union Générale d'édition, 1972). Also see, Alain Jouffroy, "Le future abolira-t-il lart?" [1970] in *L'Abolition de l'art* (Falaise: Impeccables, 2011), 75–83.

24   Jouffroy, *L'Abolition de l'art*, 15, 21.

25   Tani, "Alain Jouffroy," 390.

26   Jouffroy, *L'Abolition de l'art*, 37.

27   Ibid., 13–14.

For Jouffroy in the Givaudan Gallery essay, the abolition of art occurs when a work of art in any medium "articulates an extreme thought," thereby breaking down the limits of art and making the viewer forget that what they are confronting is a "wall" erected "between contemplation and action, theory and practice."[28] Abolishing the category of art, as just another form of "currency" ("L'ARgenT"), and with it, the world-infiltrating paradigm of the museum, will make us more aware of the "conditions of our existence."[29] Those who produce works of art are just as alienated and exploited as any other kind of worker, Jouffroy claims.[30] In contrast, "any work that does not articulate extreme thought is reducible to art and, therefore, is neutralized."[31] It is in the works and thought of Sade, Lautréamont, Fourier, Stirner, Bataille, Artaud, *and* Breton, that there is something irreducible, Jouffroy claims, something that "escapes art" and cannot be "assimilated by the cultural systems of our societies."[32] Understanding the way in which the work of these authors, and that of visual producers such as Marcel Duchamp, abolishes the concept of art, has the potential to remove the currently "derisory" associations from the label "avant-garde" as a false form of radicalism.[33] To abolish art is to move into unhindered action, to invent modes for actual change.

---

28   Ibid., 16, 33.

29   Ibid., 7, 23, 35. On the subject of the colonising powers of the museum, Jouffroy writes, "I am waiting for the day when…we will decorate the cells of prisoners condemned to death." Ibid., 7.

30   Ibid., 35.

31   Ibid., 15.

32   Ibid., 15.

33   Ibid., 16.

Jouffroy's "What's To Be Done About Art?" (1968)

In *L'Abolition de l'art*, published less than a year before the events of *Mai '68*, Jouffroy briefly introduces his concept of "revolutionary individualism," although he does not define it explicitly. He also indicates his support of the communist state of Cuba as an example of a model society.[34] A political poster in support of the Cuban Revolution is featured in the short film, *L'Abolition de l'art*, which was made in February and March of 1968 on the occasion of Pommereulle's exhibition at Givaudan Gallery. Jouffroy's narration for the film mentions a letter written to him by André Breton in 1965, shortly before Breton's death, which discusses the brevity and hardship of life, thus further linking the film to the text of the Givaudan catalogue.[35]

Eleven months later, in August of 1968, energized by the revolutionary events in Paris that spring which he calls "this abortive fourth revolution," Jouffroy wrote "Que faire de l'art?: de l'abolition de l'art à l'individualisme révolutionnaire," an expansion upon the earlier essay.[36] A new idea is introduced in this second essay: the art strike as a preliminary tactic in the process of the total abolition of art in a revolutionized society. The title, "What's To Be Done about Art," is a reference to the Marxist pamphlet authored by Vladimir Lenin in 1901-1902, *What is To Be Done? Burning Questions of Our Movement,*

---

34   Ibid., 19, 39.

35   Alain Jouffroy, "L'Abolition de l'art (film)" in *L'Abolition de l'art* (Falaise: Impeccables, 2011), 51.

36   The "fourth revolution" that Jouffroy speaks of is specifically the fourth French revolution since the late 18th century. Jouffroy, "What's To Be Done About Art?," 200.

which in itself borrowed the first part of its title from Nikolay Chernyshevsky's 1863 novel.[37]

Jouffroy's essay commences with a consideration of "intellectual producers" as "artisans of change" and "engineers of the possible" who undertake the grave task of locating "practical means" for resisting the inevitable oppression of the State.[38] He also partially defines "revolutionary individualism" as an urgent destabilizing means particularly applicable to "industrial countries that have not yet had their revolution or in which the revolution has been sabotaged."[39] Rather than relying on organized collective actions, revolutionary individualism advocates for isolated actions of resistance by lone operators, independent thought, and conscious divestiture of personal identity – which, if enacted on a mass scale, could eventually result in a "general strike throughout the world."[40]

It is only following the formation of an anti-authoritarian "counter-state" that "art" can assume new possibilities for consciousness. If "artists" join the struggle with all of the other non-artist "producers" in society in toppling State ideology, by "putting into operation...a new system of communication," then the State will gradually die.[41] As part of this process, art must be deracinated: "the primary function of the 'abolition of art' is to destroy all the cultural mythologies whereby the powers-that-be crystallize the image of their own superiority, their own intelligence; art is the armchair in

---

37   Ibid., 179, 200.

38   Ibid., 175–76.

39   Ibid., 176.

40   Ibid., 178, 198.

41   Ibid., 178.

which the State sits for its own pleasure."[42] Jouffroy exclaims, "The 'death' of the work of art, like that of God, is a piece of *luck* – it opens up all the possibilities whereby we may free ourselves from the obsession of divisive specialization."[43] Art, like any other form of capitalist production, is subject to the craft specialisation that separates workers from their products and one another.

Since Jouffroy surmises that the art establishment will continue to "believe" in the false notion of art and support all of its institutions, he agitates for the "necessity of going on an *active art strike*, using the 'machines' of the culture industry so that we can more effectively set it in *total* contradiction with itself."[44] Such an art strike cannot be merely the rejection of artists and art of the past, he explains. Rather, cultural producers must "change the most adventurous part of 'artistic' production into the production of revolutionary ideas, forms, and techniques."[45] He affirms that the only difference between his notion of the abolition of art and prior avant-garde attempts at "ideological destruction," such as that seen in dada, is that his theory of abolition "consciously and deliberately allied the elimination of esthetic values to the necessity and possibility of a social revolution."[46]

---

42   Ibid., 178.

43   Ibid., 180; emphasis original.

44   Ibid., 181; emphasis original.

45   Ibid., 181.

46   Ibid., 180.

Conclusion

Unlike his earlier essay for the Givaudan Gallery, Jouffroy mentions neither surrealism nor André Breton in the follow-up treatise "What's To Be Done About Art?" Nevertheless, the introduction of the art strike concept in the latter essay is arguably a continuation of his earlier interest in connecting surrealism, and the work of his former mentor Breton, to the revolutionary proposal for the total abolition of art supported by the cessation of the production of art in the present moment via strike. It is also clear from this subsequent essay that Jouffroy is not interested in reforming working conditions for artists and intellectuals, as was Breton in his 1925 editorial for the journal *La Révolution surréaliste*, "La Dernière grève." Whereas Breton urged the solidarity of intellectuals with the proletariat across lines of class, privilege, and craft specialisation, Jouffroy's "What's To Be Done About Art?" fundamentally levelled all workers in society to "producers" on the same plane, including the most experimental artists. Any activation of the art strike concept in Jouffroy's Marxist thought is conceived merely as a preliminary step in the transformation of cultural production and meaning as we know it. The short-lived revolution of *Mai* '68 sufficiently demonstrated to him that "art" was just another aspect of the State apparatus, and as such, it must be abolished with the rest of capitalism.

Although nowhere in Jouffroy's writings on the abolition of art or the art strike does he explicitly reference Breton's essay "La Dernière grève," the lasting influence of Breton's radical aesthetic theories about the cessation of art production in the service of societal transformation remains palpable in Jouffroy's writing on this subject into the 1970s. It is as if Breton's interwar idea of an art strike was adapted by Jouffroy for post-World War II conditions as a more fully realized *permanent* art strike, via the eradication of art in toto. In an essay written in New

York City in 1970, "Le future abolira-t-il l'art?" [Will the future abolish art?], for instance, Jouffroy weighs the short-lived nature of May 1968 and the persistence of the State despite those events, contemplating the future possibility of the realization of the abolition of art. In doing so, he revisits the theory of the "murder" of art as proposed by Breton in a 1919 letter to Tristan Tzara during the Paris dada period. There, Breton describes what Jouffroy called "the first assassination attempt on art."[47] Breton's letter states: "Killing art is what seems most urgent to me, but we will hardly be able to operate in broad daylight."[48] While Jouffroy maintains that dada failed in its sedition against art, given that dada was fully recuperated into art world institutions, he also confirms once again that threads of this radicalism survived on in the activity of someone like Duchamp. Furthermore, he designates surrealism as the avant-garde movement holding unique significance for the post-1968 moment. It is surrealism, according to Jouffroy, that enables the prefiguration of a post-revolutionary future, a "sur-realizing" of history, in which creative production enables people to "foresee the destruction of retrograde forms in our society."[49]

---

47   Jouffroy, "Le future abolira-t-il lart?," 76; author's translation. In addition to this essay, also see the chapter "Les Jacobins surrealists," in which Jouffroy makes it clear that his theory of revolutionary individualism is based on surrealism. Jouffroy, *De l'individualisme révolutionnaire*, 241–63. Jouffroy began formulating his theory of revolutionary individualism as early as 1960. See, Alain Jouffroy, "Pour un [nouvel] art révolutionnaire [vraiment] independent" [1960], Alain Jouffroy, *Les Pré-voyants* (Bruxelles: La Connaissance, 1974), 246–49.

48   Quoted in, Jouffroy, "Le future abolira-t-il lart?," 76; author's translation.

49   Ibid., 79; author's translation. Such a sentiment is echoed by Yates McKee, who describes the 2011 Occupy Wall Street movement as influenced by the "anarchist tendencies" of the "Surrealists and Situationists" in the notion of the "imagination as a creative or indeed insurrectionary force crystallized in sensuous forms... that speak to the possibility of other modes of collective life..." Yates McKee, *Strike Art: Contemporary Art and the Post-Occupy Condition* (London: Verso Books, 2016), 6.

Asynchronous Avant-Gardes: Realism in the Palestinian Revolution

Natasha Gasparian

Can an avant-garde at the so-called margins be theorized? The question tends to elicit resistance, particularly in global modern art history, a field with ever-expanding but nebulous contours. Affective responses of anxiety and suspicion typically preempt articulated critiques, signalling a disquieting lack of resolve surrounding its global legacy. When disputed in argument, the avant-garde is dismissed as an exclusionary Eurocentric term referring only to a specific set of historical movements and practices in the West – it is considered an *import* with little epistemological value. But the category "avant-garde" is fraught with a vertiginous array of competing definitions. Its primary mode of operation has been theorized, variably, as the propelling of progress;[1] the sublation of art

---

1   This earliest definition of the term was a military one. It was adapted to include the arts by Henri de Saint-Simon, a former soldier of the French revolutionary army. As Lamoureux notes, "Saint-Simon's vision for the renewal of society centered around the propelling role of a three-fold avant-garde, constituted by the scientist (*savant*), the engineer (*industriel*), and the artist, all working in concert to advance progress and prosperity in society." It echoed the utopian visions of Charles Fourier and Pierre Paul Prodhoun, and "initially competed with the romantic conception that the artist had to be free from political and social constraints (a purveyor of 'art for art's sake')." Johanne Lamoureux, "Avant-Garde: A Historiography of a Critical Concept," *A Companion to Contemporary Art Since 1945* (Oxford: Blackwell, 2006), 191–211. See also Neil McWilliam, *Dreams of Happiness. Social Art and the French Left 1830-1850* (Princeton & Oxford: Princeton University Press, 1993).

into life;[2] the mobilization of the masses; the annihilation of tradition;[3] and the myth of originality (and concomitantly, the repression of its other: repetition).[4] While there is consensus over revolution (first, the French Revolution in the nineteenth-century and then, the October Revolution early in the twentieth-century) providing the necessary conditions for its emergence in the West, the mutable theorizations of its ends and of later avant-gardes' origins and repetitions have rendered it a slippery term – almost a free-floating signifier – that can be readapted to any (non-revolutionary) context. This chapter reviews the postcolonial and decolonial reception of avant-garde historiography to reconsider the definitions operative in the rejection of the category. Positing the asynchronocity of avant-gardes as a constitutive, but historically overdetermined, feature of capitalist modernity, it aims to recover the political valence of the term and argue for its continued relevance for emancipatory struggles worldwide, notably here the ongoing struggle for the liberation of Palestine, which previously

---

2   Peter Bürger, *Theory of the Avant-Garde* (Minneapolis: University of Minnesota Press, 1984).

3   Groys claims that the contemporary reception of the Russian avant-garde concedes that mass mobilization – and the relationship between artistic revolution and political revolution in particular – is the key qualifier of an avant-garde. But this assumption, he goes on to argue, is informed by the avant-garde practices of the 1920s, which is incorrect, "because in the 1920s the Russian avant-garde was – artistically and politically – already in its post-revolutionary phase." His wager is to consider the Russian pre-revolutionary avant-garde as relevant to the contemporary situation; that is, Malevich's art of the ground zero. Boris Groys, "The Russian Avant Garde Revisited," Marc James Léger (ed.), *The Idea of the Avant-Garde and What It Means Today* (Manchester and New York: Manchester University Press, 2014), 168–75.

4   Rosalind E. Krauss, "The Originality of the Avant-Garde," *The Originality of the Avant-Garde and Other Modernist Myths* (Cambridge, MA and London: MIT Press, 1985), 151–70.

comprised a distinct movement known in Arabic as the Palestinian Revolution (1967-1982).

The Postcolonial Historicists: Synchronicity and Originality

Informed by the cultural turn within art history, early scholarship of modern art in the Arabic-speaking world sought to provide a corrective to the disciplinary assumption that non-Western art is lagging and derivative by appealing to the coevalness of "Arab"[5] art. But in so doing, it has privileged the myth of innovation as the principal – if not only – definition of the avant-garde, thus unwittingly reproducing the evolutionism and aestheticism of avant-garde historiography. In particular, Clement Greenberg's understanding of the avant-garde – a term he uses interchangeably with modernism – as a formalist tradition of high art that preserves (rather than destroys) the institution to art,[6] has set the stakes for the study of modern Arab art. Valorizing the formalist practices of the 1950-60s as exemplary of a postcolonial Arab modernism, art historians Kamal Boullata, Salwa Mikdadi, Nada Shabout and Silvia Naef have restricted their studies to artists who safeguarded tradition – "Islamic art" – from its newly assigned function as a decorative art, on the one hand, and articulated their local character and hence their

---

5   The term "Arab art" has been deployed by art historians to indicate a cultural – rather than a racial or religious – category.

6   For Greenberg, the avant-garde (as modernism) was defined by its medium-specificity – what Peter Bürger has rightly argued involves the "progressive reduction to the essential qualities of each medium," wherein art developed out of the past without a break. See Clement Greenberg, "Modernist Painting (1961)," *Modern Art and Modernism: A Critical Anthology* (Oxford: Routledge, 1982) Peter Bürger, "Avant-Garde and Neo-Avant-Garde: An Attempt to Answer Certain Critics of Theory of the Avant-Garde," *New Literary History*, vol. 40, no. 4, 2011, 698.

cultural difference from mid-twentieth century Western abstract painting, on the other.[7] In demonstrating that modern Arab artists have masterfully combined formal strategies of local traditions with ostensibly Western mediums, forms, and practices to forge distinctive postcolonial Arab identities, these historians have adopted Greenberg's pairing of the avant-garde with (and against) kitsch.[8] Shabout establishes that Arab art does not develop out of Islamic manuscript illumination or calligraphy, but is instead posited as a conscious break with an "Islamic" past. Similarly, Naef states that "Islamic art" was replaced in Arab countries by "Western art" at the end of the nineteenth and the beginning of the twentieth centuries, only to be rediscovered again (as tradition) in the second half of the twentieth century "when it became an identity issue in the art production of the Arab world."[9] For her part, Shabout restricts her account to a second generation of modernists who reacted against the academicism of a previous generation,[10] signalling a partiality to

---

7   Kamal Boullata, *Palestinian Art: From 1850 to the Present* (London: Saqi Books, 2009); Salwa Mikdadi, *Forces of Change: Artists of the Arab World* (Washington, D.C.: International Council for Women in the Arts, National Museum of Women in the Arts, 1994); Silvia Naef, *A La Recherche d'une Modernité Arabe: L'Évolution Des Arts Plastiques En Egypte, Au Liban et En Irak* (Geneva: Éditions Slatkine, 1996); Nada Shabout, *Modern Arab Art: Formation of Arab Aesthetics* (Gainesville, FL: University Press of Florida, 2007).

8   Clement Greenberg, "Avant-Garde and Kitsch," Francis Frascina (ed.), *Pollock and After: The Critical Debate* (London: Harper & Row, n.d.), 35–45. Initially published in *Partisan Review*, vol. 7, no.4, July-August 1940, 296-310.

9   Silvia Naef, "Reexploring Islamic Art: Modern and Contemporary Creation in the Arab World and Its Relation to the Artistic Past," *RES: Anthropology and Aesthetics*, no. 43: Islamic Arts, Spring 2003, 165.

10   Shabout, *Modern Arab Art*, 13–23.

Arabic Lettrist (*hurifiyya*) practices.[11] While this grouping "does not denote a unified movement or style,"[12] it stands apart from an earlier generation whose supposed mimicry of Western art renders it unworthy of the descriptor "Arab art."[13] The qualifying category of "Arab" signals an identity that was consciously "formulated in the mid-twentieth century as an ideological weapon of resistance."[14] Apart from the surrealist group *Jama'at al-Fann wa-l-Hurriyya* (Art and Freedom Group),[15] active in 1930s Egypt, the second generation is represented by artists whose practices emerged with the rise of the discourse of Arab nationalism. Implicit here is the emergence of a politically independent, self-conscious postcolonial art, but this postcolonialism is conceived within the confines of bourgeois aestheticism.

---

11   Nada Shabout, "Huroufiyah: The Arabic Letter as Visual Form," Anneka Lenssen, Sarah Rogers, and Nada Shabout (eds.), *Modern Art in the Arab World* (New York: The Museum of Modern Art, 2018), 142–43.

12   Shabout, *Modern Arab Art*, xiv.

13   Kirsten Scheid presents a more nuanced view of artistic practices during the French mandate period. Rather than accusing artists of imitation, she reveals the centrality of artmaking to the negotiation of citizenship, and agential subjectivation more broadly. Kirsten Scheid, "Necessary Nudes: Hadatha and Mu'asira in the Lives of Modern Lebanese," *International Journal of Middle East Studies*, 2010, 203–30; Kirsten Scheid, "Necessary Nudes," *Art, Awakening, and Modernity in the Middle East: The Arab Nude, 1st edition* (New York: Routledge, 2020).

14   Shabout, *Modern Arab Art*, xiv.

15   This group is often referred to in English as the Art and Liberty Group, but I opt in for the translation Art and Freedom Group, where freedom is translated from the Arabic *hurriyya*, rather than from the French *liberté*. Whereas liberty denotes a relationship between the individual subject and institutions (such as the state) that are regarded to be external to it, freedom is a speculative *a priori* category, particularly in the tradition of critique following Kant. The former connotes an atomistic understanding of the subject and maintains the antinomy between private and public, and individual and state, while the structure of the latter can arguably accommodate the Marxist and psychoanalytic notion (befitting surrealism) of an alienated, split subject whose conditions for freedom are grounded in (unconscious) human activity rather than in consciousness.

Here it is instructive to return to Bürger's stagist yet ruptural model of the avant-garde and consider its postcolonial reception. For Bürger, art developed in several stages from the sacral to the courtly, and finally, to the bourgeois in the eighteenth and nineteenth centuries. The last stage is itself divided into three phases. The first one is characterized by an increased autonomy in the sphere of aesthetics, which is historically precipitated by the shift from a reliance on patronage to the market economy. The second phase witnesses the rise of symbolism, and with it an aesthetics of "art for art's sake," wherein art divests itself from the social world, and pursues formal concerns as an end. The third and final phase is marked by the rise of what Bürger names the historical avant-garde in the aftermath of the First World War[16]. Avant-garde movements programmatically set out to attack the institutionalization of art and artistic autonomy, and to sublate art into the praxis of life. Bürger argues that these two vanguard principles mutually condition each other: the latter of the two principles, the sublation of art into life, is a goal that can only be met if it liberates art from the institutional restrictions that block its role in the social world.[17] His account reveals that the historical avant-garde was part of modernism insofar as it responded to aestheticism, but that this response constituted a break.[18] It is out of this specific contradiction that the historical avant-garde arises. Whereas Bürger argues that the avant-garde emerged from a break with bourgeois aestheticism, the historians of Arab art make a case for a postcolonial (Arab nationalist) modernism *as* aestheticism. Thus, modernism assumes the bourgeois, albeit syncretic, character of aestheticism out

---

16   For Bürger, the historical avant-garde was made up solely of the movements of Dada, Surrealism, and Constructivism (and other related Soviet experiments, such as Productivism). Peter Bürger, *Theory of the Avant-Garde.*

17   Ibid., 49.

18   Ibid.

of a break with a belated, mimetic academicism. Art historians have generalized their claims on modernism based on their analyses on specific culture and identity debates in art. For example, whereas The Baghdad Modern Art Group who actively sought to cultivate a postcolonial national identity through the interweaving of images, motifs, and symbols in Iraqi cultural tradition (*turath*) – namely, in 13th century manuscript art – with what they considered to be Western *styles* of modern art, militant artists, such as Aref El Rayess, insisted that Lebanon had no specific heritage upon which to base a postcolonial artistic style or identity. El Rayess explicitly stated that "we in Lebanon do not have any of these fixed norms that guarantee the future of art and thought through its consolidation and nationalization."[19] Moreover, the art historical preoccupation with tradition and authenticity (*asala*) risks de-historicizing works of art by uncritically reproducing the modern Arab artists' existentialist and nationalist articulation of authenticity. In a move more conservative than Peter Bürger's own widely criticized, narrowly historicist, view of the avant-garde project as a failed punctual event, Arab art historiography has dislodged the avant-garde from its revolutionary ambitions entirely.

The Decolonial Nominalists: De-territoriality and Multiplicity

The decolonial rebuttal to historicist analyses of modernism has undertaken the displacement of avant-garde origins from

---

19   Aref El-Rayess, "Rusum Thatiyya," Ibrahim Al-Salahi (ed.), *Hiwar*, no. 26–27, April 1967, 141–61. Baghdad Group for Modern Art, "Manifesto," Anneka Lenssen, Sarah Rogers, and Nada Shabout (eds.), *Modern Art in the Arab World*; Natasha Gasparian, "The Committed Artist," *Commitment in the Artistic Practice of Aref El-Rayess: The Changing of Horses* (London and New York: Anthem Press, 2020), 17–31.

their supposed Western centers as its primary aim, challenging the attachment to the paradigm of authenticity in previous postcolonial interventions within global modern art history. Prita Meier observes that this paradigm results in a tension between the local and the global, or more pointedly, between particularity and universality (she describes this as "the authenticity paradox").[20] At stake for Meier in these art historical accounts of cultural difference is their reliance upon the West/non-West binary; they remain mired with Eurocentric norms and values,[21] from which local experiences of colonial and pre-colonial encounters and systems of knowledge are to be liberated. She calls into question the very analytic categories of modernism and modernity for "uphold[ing] the West as normative center," and accordingly, "demand[ing] a teleology of artistic originality."[22] She instead proposes to "contextualize cultural practices in more precise localities, but also to seek to capture how artistic practices are claim-making strategies within a shifting web of new and old forms of territoriality."[23] The (escapist) tendency to jettison the categories of modernism and modernity has seen global art historians turn to networks of cross-cultural interaction in concrete spaces like the sea where multiple temporalities converge on a single

---

20   Prita Meier, "Authenticity and Its Modernist Discontents: The Colonial Encounter and African and Middle Eastern Art History," *The Arab Studies Journal* 18, no. 1: "Visual Arts and Art Practices in The Middle East," Spring 2010, 18-21.

21   Ibid., 19.

22   Ibid.

23   Ibid., 36.

spatial plane.[24] This gesture betrays a romantic, and ultimately impossible, fantasy of capturing moments or places that lie beyond capitalist exchange relations, and therefore outside of modernity altogether. But the categories of modernism and modernity are entangled with the totalizing logic of capitalism from which there is no outside, not even in language or discourse (commodities have agency in our topsy-turvy world; they speak, or rather, we are spoken for through them).

Postcolonial and decolonial theories fail, in sum, in their reduction of historical process and social relations to a question of discourse and representation. Symptomatically, the concrete image of the sea serves as an inadequate stand-in for the abstractions mediating the various binaries they wish to escape. Decolonial discourses often rename categories of thought without rethinking their logic. This is typified in the newly circulating terms, "Global South" and "Global North," which have come to replace the Cold-War era terms, "Third World" and "First World." Symptomatic of the post-1989 'post-ideological' discourse, the former set of terms erase the connotations carried in First World (capitalist modernity), Second World (the state socialism of the Soviet Union), and the Third

---

24   The fixation on "de-territoriality," or what has been referred to as "the spatial turn," in global art history has largely been informed by the work of the leading decolonial thinker Walter D. Mignolo. See Walter D. Mignolo, *Local Histories/Global Designs: Coloniality, Subaltern Knowledges, and Border Thinking*, Princeton Studies in Culture/Power/History (New Jersey: Princeton University Press, 2000); Walter D. Mignolo, *The Darker Side of Western Modernity: Global Futures, Decolonial Options* (North Carolina: Duke University Press, 2011). For decolonial interventions in art history, see Aruna D'Souza, "Introduction," Jill H. Casid and Aruna D'Souza (eds.), *Art History: In the Wake of the Global Turn* (Williamstown, MA: Clark Art Institute, 2014), vii–xxiii; Prita Meier, "Beyond Multiple Modernities: East African Port Cities as the Space Between," *Nka: Journal of Contemporary African Art*, no. 28, May 2020, 116–25; Prita Meier, *Swahili Port Cities: The Architecture of Elsewhere*, African Expressive Cultures (Bloomington: Indiana University Press, 2016); Piotr Piotrowski, "On the Spatial Turn, or Horizontal Art History," *Umeni/Art*, vol. 56, no. 5, 2008, 378–83.

World (anticolonial socialism). The former set makes manifest the constitutive relationship of colonialism between the two entities, but it maintains from the latter a relationship of economic dependency rooted in a model of core/periphery. They also fail to account for the capitalist determination of the colonial relation, thus resulting in a new kind of provincialism – a paradox for terms with global breadth. The shift from core to Global North and periphery to Global South is only a linguistic substitution – or, more profoundly, a return of the repressed of modernist issues.[25] Fredric Jameson diagnoses this recurrence as paradoxical, for the end of grand narratives was presumed to have been superseded by the "postmodern condition" since Lyotard's proclamation in 1979.[26] To posit multiple modernities, he claims, is "to overlook the fundamental meaning of modernity which is that of a worldwide capitalism itself. The standardization projected by capitalist globalization in third or late stage of the system casts considerable doubt on all these pious hopes for cultural variety in a future world *colonized* by a universal market order."[27] In moving beyond the impasse of postmodernism's culturalist discourses and presentist ideology, Jameson restores the question of history to the debate, and argues for modernity's singularity – a distinctly capitalist modernity with a universalizing logic.

Rather than thinking through the temporal disjunctions within a singular capitalist modernity, global art history has taken up postcolonial and decolonial currents of thought and staged a large-scale nominalist project that functions according to a logic

---

25   Fredric Jameson, *A Singular Modernity* (London & New York: Verso, 2012), 5–6.

26   Ibid.; Jean-François Lyotard, *The Postmodern Condition: A Report on Knowledge* (Minneapolis: University of Minnesota Press, 1984).

27   Emphasis is mine. Fredric Jameson, *A Singular Modernity*. (London &New York: Verso, 2012), 6–13.

of summation – an expansion of the geographical boundaries of the canon. Multiple or alternate modernities (and consciousnesses) are posited, each with a culturally defined modernism and its set of exemplary artists.[28] Eschewing the category of the universal, the central preoccupation for global art history becomes one of the translation of cultures, or rather, their very untranslatability. Accordingly, Aruna D'Souza proposes to reimagine the discipline of art history by being attendant to "the ways in which art history is spoken differently."[29] This is at odds with her declaration that such an approach, which "thrives on misunderstandings, incommensurabilities, the misprisions of our conversations across geographies and times"[30] is disruptive of the discipline, precisely because the attention to art histories' many tongues (if they even exist) relies upon the mutual recognition of the Western subject and the non-Western Other – a process that is itself uneven and necessarily involves the former's domination of the latter, as the self-consciousness of the subject is achieved through, and at the expense of, the Other.[31] However, the self-conscious Western subject has largely been understood as an atomistic individual. Implicit here is the supposition that the speaking subject is whole, and can fully identify with its language, or, in the case of the historicists of modern Arab art, it is the supposition that the "Western" speaking subject is whole, and the art historian's task is to demonstrate the self-sufficiency of the Arab individual subject. Both postcolonial and decolonial tendencies in art history have reproduced this liberal fantasy of

---

28 For more on the seminal debates on multiple modernities, see Dilip Parameshwar Gaonkar (ed.), *Alternative Modernities* (Durham & London: Duke University Press, 2001); S.N. Eisenstadt et al., *Daedalus*, vol. 129, no. 1: "Multiple Modernities," 2000.

29 Aruna D'Souza, "Introduction", xviii.

30 Ibid.

31 Frantz Fanon, *Black Skin, White Masks* (New York: Grove Press, 1952), 163–73.

the plenitude of the atomistic subject – of an individual artist who can fully identify with oneself with no excess; an exemplar whose hybrid forms are a solution to the problems of imitation and derivativeness.[32] Decolonial theory rejects the category of the avant-garde, but it simultaneously reproduces its most enduring myth – genius.

Asynchronocity and the New Sensibility

Sidestepping the ideology of multicultural pluralism permeating the discipline, and anxieties of the artist as a postcolonial subject-supposed-to-know, the category avant-garde continues to be relevant for the study of militant art outside of the Euro-American canon. It has been taken up in the work of several scholars of Arabic literature and music who have quietly endorsed the term without always belaboring the parameters of its use or significance.[33] Paying close attention to the writers and critics who rethought the task of the intellectual amid defeat and reworked literary forms to politically engage readers and spectators, Rebecca Johnson notes that the so-called self-reflexive "inward turn" in avant-gardist

---

32 Chika Okeke-Agulu introduces the category of the "exemplary" postcolonial modernist, therefore making explicit what remains unuttered in global art historical interventions: the singularity of the postcolonial artist. See Chika Okeke-Agulu, *Postcolonial Modernism: Art and Decolonization in Twentieth-Century Nigeria* (Durham: Duke University Press, 2015).

33 The two volumes sharing the title *The Arab Avant-Garde* unhelpfully echo the nominalist drive toward multiplicity in decolonial currents. Thomas Burkhalter, Kay Dickinson, and Benjamin J. Harbert, *The Arab Avant-Garde: Music, Politics, Modernity* (Middletown, Connecticut: Wesleyan University Press, 2013); Andrea Flores Khalil, *The Arab Avant-Garde: Experiments in North African Art and Literature.* (Westport, Connecticut: Praeger, 2003); Rebecca Johnson, "Cross-Revolutionary Reading: Visions of Vietnam in the Transnational Avant-Garde," *Comparative Literature*, vol. 73, no. 3, 2021, 360–81.

literature following 1967 – what was dubbed "the New Sensibility" (*al-hassassiyya al-jadida*) – was also an outward move, not only an orientation toward local concerns and struggles but also to those further afield: the Palestinian Revolution and its intersections with causes elsewhere, including, notably, the fight against war in Vietnam.[34] Yet while researchers have contextualized the liberation of Palestine within global solidarity movements in the long 1960s,[35] they have failed to account for the specificity of the avant-gardism of the New Sensibility and its singular though asynchronous appearance thirty years after the practices local militant artists cited as models for their commitment, such as Mexican Muralism and Brechtian theatre. For the next fifteen years – until the Palestinian Liberation Organization (PLO) was forced out of Beirut in 1982 during the Israeli siege of Beirut and the Sabra and Shatila Massacres in the Palestinian refugee camps – artists and writers turned to realism as an aesthetic and political program appropriate to their revolutionary ambitions. Realism was mobilized not as a style but a *method*. The new sensibility was not – as is commonly thought – simply a resigned, self-reflexive, (post-)modernist response to the preceding decades' existentialist committed literature (realism *as* art – a style – rather than realism as operative method).[36] Contrary to the historiographical consensus that the Arab

---

34   Ibid. 361.

35   See Kristine Khouri and Rasha Salti, *Past Disquiet: Artists, International Solidarity, and Museums-in-Exile*, The Museum Under Construction 15 (Warsaw: Museum of Modern Art in Warsaw, 2018) and Zeina Maasri, *Cosmopolitan Radicalism: The Visual Politics of Beirut's Global Sixties*, The Global Middle East 13 (Cambridge: Cambridge University Press, 2020).

36   See John Robert's contribution in "Realism Today?," *ARTMargins*, Roundtable, vol. 7, no. 1, 2018, 61–62; Fredric Jameson, *The Antinomies of Realism* (London & New York: Verso, 2013).

defeat of the war effected historical rupture – often conflated with a paradigm shift – the demise of Nasser and the Arab armies did not lead to the disenchantment of the Arab left *tout court*. Like the Western art historians Peter Bürger, Hal Foster and John Roberts, who premised their theories of the neo-avant-garde on the neoliberal foreclosure of emancipatory politics following May 1968 (and the fall of the Berlin Wall later in 1989), historians and scholars of Arabic literary studies have taken the expressions of defeat following the June 1967 War at face value. In disregarding the distinction between an epistemological break and transformations on the level of the mode of production – and, specifically, whether the former was an effect of the latter – the treatment of the war has largely reified the Arab defeat, not least because artists and intellectuals publicly articulated their refusal to assume it as their own.

In the aftermath of June 1967, the editors of two literary magazines long considered to belong to opposing camps, Adonis (editor of the formalist *Shi'r* [poetry]) and Suhail Idriss (editor of the committed al-Adab [The Arts and Letters]), penned similarly ardent editorials against the ensuing sense of fatalism on the left. Idriss intervened in the thicket of gloom by calling on the Arab writer to take on the role of the fida'i – a freedom fighter for the Palestinian cause – in their struggle against the reactionary forces of imperialism and Zionism. Rather than take up arms, Idriss called on them to "weaponize the word" in order to fulfill the dual task of mobilizing a crowd of readers by nurturing in them a combatant energy, and to fight the "campaigns" of defeat put forward by "hired journalists and mercenary *'udaba* (men of letters)." As a militant intellectual, the writer was to put up a steadfast front against the conservative forces of neocolonialism, and in so doing, serve as a leader – an ideal model – to readers.[37]

Similarly, Adonis's editorial in the inaugural issue of *Mawaqif* (positions) – a little magazine founded as a direct response to the June War – claimed to preempt resignation by serving as its determinate negation. "Welcom[ing] the unknown and wad[ing] its entrails," it advanced a militant understanding of culture: "Culture, here, is struggle – the unity of thought, as well as work. It does not concern itself with explaining the world, life, or the human, but rather, seeks to transform them. Culture – revolution."[38]

Both political declarations – manifestos in their own right – attest to the persistence and radicalization of the discourse of commitment (rather than its eclipse) in the two camps, blurring the divide between them. In the years that followed, commitment was reformulated within a language of revolutionary mass politics and reconfigured through new forms of artmaking. By 1970, artist and intellectual Kamal Boullata discerned a shift toward realism following the June War – a shift, he argues, does not simply introduce figuration or a change in iconography, but cultivates an entirely new sensibility. Precipitated by a reevaluation of the artist's revolutionary role, he observes that: "[s]ome poets exchanged their typewriters for machine guns; others abandoned poetry to write novels and those who formerly wrote love poems turned to social and political themes. The experimental moviemaker became the mere photographer of events for documentary purposes.

---

37   Suhayl Idriss, "Al-Adib fi-l-Ma'raka!," *al-Adab*, no. 6, June 1967, 1–2. For an English translation of Idriss' editorial, see Natasha Gasparian, *Commitment in the Artistic Practice of Aref El-Rayess: The Changing of Horses* (London: Anthem Press, 2020), 21.

38   Adonis, "Editorial," *Mawaqif*, no. 1, October 1968, 3–4.

A professional painter became a graphic artist, an illustrator, or a social worker…To meet the new Arab man that the Palestinian revolution is in the process of creating, Palestinian art cannot seek reforms, but rather new forms."[39] As Boullata suggests, the new sensibility (as both the name of militant art after 1967 and the new mode of perception it inspired) took on a multitude of appearances in painting, theatre, film, and literature that assumed both demystifying and defamiliarizing functions (the former thought to be a function of realism; the latter, modernism), often prompting encounters in readers and spectators – in little magazines, large-scale paintings, films, and portable works on paper and posters – that had the capacity to restructure perception. Importantly, the term "New Sensibility" was not a retrospective designation imposed on artistic and literary production in Beirut in the late 1960s but was itself avowed by artists in countless manifestos. A close corollary, "New Vision," (Ru'ya Jadida) was put forth by a group of Iraqi artists who refuted the embalming of the past and called for a break with tradition to create it, and the world, anew. Art's role, as they defined it, was not "merely a mirror of the artist's lived reality, but also the spirit of the future."[40] Rejecting any identification with the defeat and taking the street as the site of encounter, they asserted their support of, and participation in the "popular war of liberation."[41]

---

39   First published in Kamal Boullata, "Nahwa Fan Arabi Thawri," *Mawaqif*, no. 9, June 1970, 26–44. For the full English translation, see Kamal Boullata, "Toward a Revolutionary Arab Art," Finbarr Barry Flood (ed.), *There Where You Are Not: Selected Writings of Kamal Boullata* (Munich: Hirmer, 2019).

40   The New Vision group was founded in 1969 and included Iraqi artists Dia al-Azzawi, Ismail Fattah, Saleh al-Jumaie, Muhmmad Muhraddin, Rafa al-Nasiri, and Hashem Samarchi. For the full English version of their manifesto, see Dia al-Azzawi et al., "Manifesto: Towards a New Vision," Anneka Lenssen, Sarah Rogers, and Nada Shabout (eds.), *Modern Art in the Arab World*, 308.

41   Ibid. 309.

In the Arabic-speaking world of the mid-twentieth century, there was no aesthetic *and* political avant-garde without the Palestinian Revolution. In the aftermath of 1967, artists committed themselves to the struggle for socialism with the Palestinian cause serving as a global conduit through the satellite of Beirut. Despite the divergence in medium, format and style across artistic practices, this avant-garde was bound by a realist *method* and a common cause. Yet this art has not made it into the global artistic canon – neither, paradoxically, via the postcolonial and decolonial art historiography and contemporary exhibition-making practices, nor the local, and decidedly nationalist art historical accounts. As the art of the Palestinian Revolution, it has not entered the canon because it gave shape to – and was shaped by – a national liberation struggle that was (and still is) the repressed underside of the Lebanese Wars (1975–90).[42] The class-based struggle over political hegemony and regional economic interests is still often misinterpreted because of its sectarian appearance (a war between Christian and Muslim communities). The traces of the struggle have been retroactively erased since its defeat in 1982.

This is perhaps why the art of the Palestinian Revolution is precluded from John Roberts' sophisticated theorization of revolutionary time and the avant-garde. Like Hal Foster who regards the avant-garde as traumatic to the symbolic sphere in which it intervenes and, having been partly repressed, returns from the future,[43] Roberts theorizes the avant-garde in relation to revolutionary time as constituting irruptions and cuts in historical time (rather than shifting from time to space,

---

42   The Lebanese Wars, more commonly known as the Lebanese Civil War, were a multifaceted series of conflicts among a pro-Western government, Christian nationalist militias, and pro-Palestinian, pan-Arabist, leftist, and later Muslim armed groups.

43   Hal Foster, "What's Neo About the Neo Avant-Garde," *October*, no. 70, 1994, 31.

as though the two were separable. Time, too, can be colonized[44]). But in his attempt to postulate the universal reach of the avant-garde, he singles out a manifesto on Arab Surrealism, written in 1975 (the year of the start of the wars), as an instance of a belated transnational avant-garde.[45] In doing so he problematically retains a core/periphery model and overemphasizes the conscious reworking of the historical avant-garde's "core program." The one-off example he cites merely serves to point to the existence of the avant-garde in spaces and times beyond Western Europe, but it is misleading not least because surrealism had long lost its political verve everywhere and had become inextricable from reified spectacle. In Lebanon, it was totally enmeshed within the gallery circuit, partly through the network of the commercial gallery *Centre d'Art*, set up by poet Georges Schehade and his wife Brigitte. The Schehades hosted Marx Ernst and Dorothea Tanning in Beirut, sold prints by surrealists Ernst, Leonor Fini, André Masson, Paul Éluard and others, and exhibited paintings and works on paper by local artists Cici Sursock, Juliana Seraphim and George Doche, who had taken up surrealism as a style rather than a set of techniques. In the Beirut of the 1970s, surrealism had been entirely subsumed within the sphere of bourgeois enjoyment.[46] It would perhaps suffice to recognize, as Geeta Kapur does,

---

44   Susan Buck-Morss, *Year 1: A Philosophical Recounting* (Cambridge, Massachusetts: MIT Press, 2021), x.

45   Abdul Kadar El-Janaby, Fadil Abas Hadi, Farid Lariby, Faroq El-Juridy, Ghazi Younis, and Maroin Dib. "Manifesto of the Arab Surrealist Movement, 1975," *Arsenal: Surrealist Subversion*, no. 3, 1976, online at: https://theanarchistlibrary.org/library/various-authors-surrealism-in-the-arab-world cited in John Roberts, *Revolutionary Time and the Avant-Garde* (London and New York: Verso, 2015), 40.

46   For more on surrealism in 1970s Beirut, see Natasha Gasparian, "The Trouble with Sex: Surrealism as Style in 1970s Beirut," *Beirut and the Golden Sixties* (Milan: Silvana Editoriale, 2022), 32–37.

the Soviet Union's revolutionary phase as an *originary* (rather than original) moment for the avant-garde without claiming direct lineages in practice. In her manifesto-like proposition for an avant-garde in the Global South, Kapur claims that the Soviet art of the 1920s "remains *the* historical avant-garde of the 20th century, but with the social transformations wrought by successive waves of decolonization peaking around the mid-twentieth century," "the avant-garde principle, as defined by 20th century western art, was substantially, *tendentially*, altered."[47] She cites Fanon, the poetics of Négritude, the Indian People's Theatre Association, and Third Cinema from Latin America. To be added to her list is the realism of the Palestinian Revolution.

The Palestinian Revolution demands art historical attention. To regard it historically and materially is to challenge the evolutionist historicism of the ideology of the avant-garde – modernity as the teleological progression of history, advancement in modernization processes as favourable conditions for revolution, and the modern artwork as "advanced" – and that of postcolonial and decolonial theory, which presumes the West to be the locus from which modernity emerges and then spreads. Its anachronism cannot be explained as the material consequence of uneven power relations between the West and rest of the world. Instead, to make sense of its untimely character, it is imperative to grasp the totalizing structure of capitalism. Critical reevaluations of totality in the Hegelian system reveal that it cannot be understood as a process that ends in union and synchronicity. Its asymmetry is structurally

---

47 Geeta Kapur, "Proposition Avant-Garde: A View from the South," *Art Journal*, vol. 77, no. 1, 2018, 87–89.

constitutive (but historically overdetermined).[48] Capitalist modernity, as the historically overdetermined model of our social totality, is a singular but uneven historical process. It is internally contradictory and asynchronous, rather than oppositional to another, culturally defined modernity. Slavoj Žižek explains that its asynchronicity is "ultimately not only the delay between the elements of the same historical totality, but the delay of the totality with regard to itself, the structural necessity for a totality to contain anachronistic elements which alone make it possible for it to establish itself as a totality – is the temporal aspect of a gap which propels the dialectical process…"[49] It would therefore be futile to record moments of synchronicity among places, people, and artistic forms, or to yearn for the ostensible end point in which these all converge. The art historical task is rather to grapple with the structural asynchronicity and asymmetry within the social totality.

---

48   Rebecca Comay, *Mourning Sickness: Hegel and the French Revolution*, Cultural Memory in the Present (Stanford: Stanford University Press, 2010), 125, cited in Slavoj Žižek, *Less Than Nothing: Hegel and The Shadow of Dialectical Materialism*, 2nd ed. (London & New York: Verso, 2013), 439.

49   Ibid., 438.

A Future Everyone Can Get Behind

Marina Vishmidt

As I prepare my contribution to this edited collection, I may not have an insight into the other chapters but feel I can assert with a fair degree of confidence that the observation that 'avant-garde' is an untimely category will not be mine alone. It seems, rather, to be a caveat incumbent on anyone planning to do substantive work with that category. How avant-garde as a noun and as an adjective became untimely doesn't need to be rehearsed at great length, as the winds in art, cultural and political theory have long been blowing contrary to the notion of progress stipulated in it, perhaps ever since those winds turned against the angel of history. It seems somewhat paradoxical, that you can go against a time that is no longer moving in a straight line, but it is of course possible to go against *an orthodoxy* that time does not move in a straight line; or, the presumption that this is a question that has been settled.

What was the avant-garde, then? It was a military metaphor that positioned the arts ahead of society, and certain artists and movements ahead of others. It was a category that was retired in the face of a pluralism that could no longer entertain the thought of some being ahead and some being behind, as this presupposed one linear, hegemonic narrative. End of story. A more involved and generative reading, such as the one undertaken by Peter Osborne (2013) includes the category of avant-garde in a philosophical argument about modernism's temporal politics, positing that the avant-garde was the determinate negation of the past by art – a future-oriented temporality as an *overcoming* – as opposed to a more abstract, formal relationship to the future entertained by the general category of modernism. More recently, Osborne has proposed that the 'contemporary' – all times at once and in coexistence – is the imprint of the heterogeneous temporality of dominant global capital on the worldview and institutions of art. The slippage between the avant-garde operating as a category of temporality and a category of periodization in Osborne's work over the past decades looks to a resolution, if provisional, in the category of the contemporary, since as an index of the totalization of the experience of time by capital, the dimension of futurity inextricable from the idiom of the avant-garde is marginalised, or removed (again, tendentially). This echoes Peter Bürger's 'theory of the avant-garde,' where the avant-garde is seen as the reflexive movement in modern art that sought to change or eliminate art in its larger undertaking to see the world transformed. Once the horizons of that ambition deflate to the precincts of art itself, become art-immanent, as in his chronology of the post WW2 Western art, what you get is the neo-avant garde – call it 'contemporary art' – which hollowly reiterates the constructivist gestures but not the political reach, of the pre-war avant-gardes of e.g. Dadaism (the reference frame is Western and capitalist, because in this account the avant-garde trajectory was curtailed earlier and more decisively by Soviet socialist realism). So here already there are two dislocations. First, the avant-garde moves from the literal battlefield to the battlefield of culture, signalling an 'advanced detachment' that no longer seeks out the enemy but rather the new, making an enemy of the old. It runs to stay ahead of not only the culture industry or 'kitsch' (Greenberg) but of modern art itself, engaged in a never-halting Oedipal treadmill that became the hegemonic image for white male modernism.[1] Even where it refuses that myth and that habitus, it is still in the same race, as in the 'realization and supersession of art' spoken of by the Situationists. Second, the avant-garde is dislocated in time, always somewhere other than where it is, pulling the future into the present. This dislocation is in many ways constitutive of the 'future presencing' ontology of the avant-garde in 20th century art (even its ties to spiritualism can be seen as a sort of invocation 'out of time'). Such a dislocation will be explored more closely later in the text. At the same time, it should also be understood as that future-facing element of cultural production that has seen the avant-garde as the fount of innovation for the 'culture industry,' which itself can be deemed the 'research and development' wing of capital, as Thomas Crow noted nearly thirty years ago.[2]

---

1   Although there is a robust current of analysis in the literature that suggests – akin to the disputed nature of 'universalism' in contemporary left political theory – that the modernist project, in all its multiplicity, should be distinguished from hegemonic capitalist and imperialist 'modernization.' For an example of this discussion, see Kanishka Goonewardena's "Space" in the *SAGE Handbook of Marxism*: "The withering away of the revolution rather than the state or capital [...] robbed radical modernism of its essential political dimension, leaving art and technology in a state that made them liable to rapid cooptation by capital and the 'state mode of production,' upon the Stalinization of the Soviet bloc and the consolidation of what Gramsci called 'Americanism and Fordism' in the overdeveloped capitalist world. The result of that was modernization, not modernism." Kanishka Goonewardena, "Space," Beverley Skeggs, Sara R. Farris, Alberto Toscano and Svenja Bromberg (eds.), *SAGE Handbook of Marxism* (London: Sage, 2021), 520. This discussion thus re-maps the distinction between 'modernism' (hegemonic) and 'avant-garde' (radical) in the historical ontology of art in modernity traced by Osborne above, as well as others.

2   Thomas Crow, *Modern Art in the Common Culture* (New Haven: Yale University Press, 1996), 35.

Gain-of-Function Avant-Garde?

But it does also seem evident that there is only so far such a dislocation can go if the model of time remains linear and progressive, even if the monolithic conception of a unified time moving forward that continues to represent the 'ideal-typical' temporality of Western modernism (with the two terms often so identified that the combination can sound pleonastic) was full of returns, selective revivals, 'invented traditions' and the challenges to the assumptions of the forward march of progress, such as the one outlined by Walter Benjamin as 'messianic time.' Nonetheless, the kind of closer scrutiny to a hegemonically linear schema of modernity that can be identified with such challenges show us that the schema was never uncontested, and that its contestations carried political implications. Certainly the avant-garde as a concept or position cannot be dissociated from the existence of a vanguard party and vanguardism. These are to be understood as a concerted socialist politics and its organisational correlate in the Party tasked with effecting the movement into an emancipatory future for society, with the Party as both the expressive organ and the representative of the exploited majorities of capitalist, postcolonial or semi-feudal societies over a large part of the globe and for most of the duration of the 20th century. Vanguardism as a perspective in leftist politics was not confined to the mass electoral parties, as often formations and currents to the left of these organisations decried their bureaucratic character and claimed the terrain of the real 'vanguard,' the really advanced position in both analysis and strategy, of the movement.

Once these political co-ordinates melted away in the last half century loosely defined as the neoliberal era, the temporality defined by the forward motion of emancipation, however uneven, could no longer be legitimated in art either. No doubt the avant-garde had always been a fissile tendency in Western modernism, with social revolution and aesthetic revolution often programmatically parting ways, as with the Greenbergian and Friedian formalisms, to take just one, provincial example. The dismantling of linear temporality in the humanities and social sciences (also the physical ones) with post-modernism, structuralism, and post-structuralism, also ensured that avant-garde precepts became both unfashionable and untenable in cultural theory and art education. Institutional mutations aside, the loss of an avant-garde horizon seems indisputable; the avant-garde is now primarily discussed in historical terms, not as something that can be actualised today. Its fading from consequence seems to have an ethical, as much as a political, valence. How is it possible to assert that something is more valuable because it is 'advanced,' when the universalism that would give meaning to such a valuation has itself been so comprehensively discredited? It should be noted, however, that in the recent decade, the category of the avant-garde has made a minor comeback in the precincts of Marxist art history, with scholars such as John Roberts and Angela Dimitrakaki writing cogently on a 'suspensive' avant-garde that retains the promise of art's non-identity with global capital's forces and ideologies of production and an 'avant-garde horizon' that does not affirm the existence of a contemporary avant-garde but its possibility as a space of struggle in institutions, respectively.[3] The ambition here seems to be precisely to make a cut with the shapeless complicity of 'contemporary art' in Osborne's symptomatic reading in favour of rehabilitating a positive theoretical category for artistic practices that see themselves as continuous with political activism and

---

3   John Roberts, *Revolutionary Time and the Avant-Garde* (Verso: New York and London, 2015); see also John Roberts, "Revolutionary Pathos, Negation and the Suspensive Avant-Garde," *New Literary History*, vol. 41, no. 4, 2010, 717-730; Angela Dimitrakaki, "The Avant-Garde Horizon: Socially Engaged Art, Capitalism and Contradiction," paper presented at *Socially Engaged Practice: Aesthetics, Politics or Economics?*, 3 March, CCA Glasgow in the context of the exhibition curated by Dimitrakaki and Kirsten Lloyd, *ECONOMY*.

education but also 'autonomous' in the sense that they don't get folded into the colonial schemes of social betterment that often unfolds under the aegis of 'social engagement' and 'social practice' but instead see themselves as part of a global anti-oppressive and hopefully, anti-capitalist, re-composition and struggle.

While there is a felt necessity to approach cultural practice for the concrete universality it can offer rather than the bad infinity of pluralism that accounts for politics as a shifting moodboard that enjoins 'keeping up' with particular grammars and concerns season from season, the forward-facing temporality of the 'avant-garde' can be a non sequitur. Emancipation is a concrete universal in the sense that it is a unity-in-difference of many historical realities and speculative tendencies, and is mediated through nature, labour, culture, and many other layers of experience, thought and production. This is to be contrasted to the *abstract* universality which ignores and negates specificity and particularities. My contention here is that the political in art is a concrete universal; the 'avant-garde' is an abstract one, however dense its accumulated (Western) historical and aesthetic meanings.

An advancing line from the past into the future which is magnetized by a form of liberation or enlightenment 'up ahead,' like the 'arc that bends towards justice,' seems like a spatio-temporal figure, which is familiar in the imaginary of emancipation, but is not necessary for the concept to make sense. It is naturalised by its long-term presence as a feature of a progressive modernist narrative, but it surely cannot be the case that jettisoning the forward arrow inseparable from the concept of the 'avant-garde' means jettisoning politics, or more specifically, revolutionary desire, from cultural and aesthetic practice. Granted, the avant-garde may part ways with modernist ideas of semi-automated progress, and in fact may define itself through this break, showing instead an affinity with the rupture in time and the emergency 'brake' that Benjamin's Theses on the Philosophy of History counterposes to the disastrous complacency attending such ideas. Yet in upholding the perspective of being 'out in front,' the 'avant-garde' retains a commitment to a provincial and reductive paradigm of transformation, as well as who its subjects and targets might be. Out in front of what? However nuanced the recent defences of 'avant-garde' might be, I would argue that those good intentions have no need of the encumbrances the term can't help dragging with it. The following section will attempt a more involved exegesis of the problem, latterly with reference to recent theoretical debates and artistic projects.

Problematic Time(s)

Scholarly and art-critical discourse has in recent years, or perhaps for longer, been working with notions of time that would seem to preclude reference to the avant-garde as anything but historic. Such notions would include, as already noted, the very definition of the 'contemporary' in contemporary art, pegged to a simultaneous rather than progressive or future-oriented temporality. A diversity of 'chronopolitics' has been at issue in much feminist and queer theory, black studies, affect theory and a number of the approaches that have been grouped under the heading 'new materialisms.' Theorists such as Heather Love or Elizabeth Freeman, drawing also on the influential work of Eve Kosofsky Sedgwick and Ann Cvetkovich, have been advancing ways of conceiving temporality, especially in literary theory and archival practice, as directly affect-laden (a 'feeling backward' in Love's terms), repairing and rescuing lost or buried figures and relations through a kind of trans-temporal intimacy. This work steadfastly refuses what Freeman defined as 'chrononormativity,' a productivist and standardizing notion of time that oppresses those who don't conform, arguing for the inextricability of 'sexual and temporal dissidence' that allows the past, in a kind of post-Benjaminian way, to spark connections with the present through a recognition of such dissidence between queered subjects across time and space. Freeman has also coined another resonant concept, 'temporal drag,' which, in common with the more uncompromising analysis of someone like Lee Edelman, counters discourses of progressive or 'reproductive' futurity with the friction of unresolved pasts of violence and marginalization on the imaginary of emancipated presents and futures. There is a sense, however, that the salience of affect in these formulations, particularly affects of ambivalence, failure, and fragment, can become a placeholder for a narrowness of vision and a lacuna of political thinking (and affect).There is thus a turning-away from the totality carried in a progressivist concept of time like the one implicated in the avant-garde, towards an all-too-familiar post-everything melancholy which dissipates any feeling of urgency or deepening contradiction. There is thus a question to be asked whether these ways of re-thinking linear, developmental time are adequate for an era in which escalating geophysical collapse and the brutality of social violence alike require action as totalizing as the scale of those events and the necrotizing force of the capitalism, imperialism, and racism that reproduces them.

While such biopolitical figurations of temporality have been prominent in queer theory, black studies have also concentrated on non-normative temporality, at times by deploying intramural idioms such as 'Colored People Time,' as in the eponymous exhibition at the MIT List Visual Arts Centre that opened during the first wave of the pandemic in early 2020. The notion of appropriating and re-purposing racially coded ascriptive difference in relation to time – slower, less efficient – is perhaps less familiar in the art context than the vast itinerary of cultural practices described as 'Afro-futurism,' a label that has been around for several decades already and which, rather than redefining a 'lack' in relation to time, posits a distinct 'surplus' yielded by the alienation and abstraction of black populations in a world of white supremacist, patriarchal capitalism. While 'Afrofuturism' has been arguably hollowed out as a useful category by overuse and overbranding, and has been slyly detourned by artists such as Martine Syms, with her 'Manifesto for a Mundane Afrofuturism' or Aria Dean's 'Blaccelerationism,' it is the Black Quantum Futurism project, comprising musician and poet Camae Ayewa and lawyer Rasheedah Phillips. It probably represents the most developed and complex re-thinking of progressive temporality from the standpoint of political aesthetics coming out of a black radical tradition[4] and quantum physics, which in recent years has infiltrated cultural theory through the work of thinkers like Karen Barad, Carlo Rovelli or, from a slightly different angle, the 'perspectivism' of the anthropologists Déborah Danowski and Eduardo Viveiros de Castro, with their re-orientation of anthropocentrism on the basis of Amazonian epistemology. Black Quantum Futurism's emphasis on subjective and cyclical notions of time foreground how (racial) capitalism exerts claims on time as well as resources and space, and that quantum mechanics can help flesh out productive, creative, and political methods to help subjugated populations, such as black people in poor urban areas in American cities, operate in such an overdetermined field to secure their own futures. Operating across scales, from a community advice centre in Philadelphia where creative workshops as well as anti-gentrification organising happens, to a residency at the CERN laboratory, the

---

4   As David Lloyd has written, "the black radical tradition is (above all) an aesthetic tradition… black music – by extension, black aesthetic practice in general – *is* and cannot be separated from black radicalism, even by so slight a difference as resemblance entails." David Lloyd, *Under Representation: The Racial Regime of Representation* (New York: Fordham University Press, 2020), 79.

collective offer a possible scenario of how a practice that in another era could have been well described as avant-garde has relinquished progressivist temporality but retained and extended its political ambition.

Likewise, a politicised and oppositional creative paradigm, albeit one that intervenes in the hegemony of space rather than time, can be discerned in the 15th Documenta, curated by ruangrupa and multiple other collectives and groups. It is perhaps in this context that we can see the most incisive divergence between the temporal logic of the avant-garde and a spatial challenge to a European hegemony of 'advanced art.' The mediator between time and space here is colonialism, and it is colonial and imperial logics that made a magnanimous invitation to the 'Global South' to come and sustain the expiring project of a Western metropolitan avant-garde in the shape of the quinquennial art festival, however nominally global in its roster of artists. As has been extensively detailed elsewhere, the "narcissistic wound" this occasioned for the German state and cultural field was clearly underestimated, and the resulting backlash, taking on both blatant and insidious forms of racism and a largely confected anti-semitism scandal that projected historical and very actual German pathologies laser-like on its unwanted non-white interlocutors was as revealing as it was abject, but it could also be understood as a reaction of outrage to the impugning of the rightful heritage of the avant-garde as an aesthetic and political principle that was the wholly-owned property of an enlightened West.[5] An approach that had developed in the wake of unyielding Western extraction and imperial marginality used social and cultural infrastructures, as well as aesthetic grammars, that broke down the art/

---

5   Ana Teixeira Pinto and Kerstin Stakemeier, "A Brief Glossary of Social Sadism," *Texte zur Kunst*, no. 116, December 2019; https://www.textezurkunst.de/en/116/brief-glossary-social-sadism/

politics binary differently, often into insignificance. This could not be tolerated, not only because with this infrastructural emphasis the 'lumbung' sidestepped the problematic of the relation between 'art' and 'politics' or 'art' and 'the social' which had long become ossified as a real question for 'contemporary art' but because they were not even interested in the terms. Such a slight to the 'master's house' was decried as an absence of 'reflexivity,' at the very least, and an unwanted revival of 'relational aesthetics,' at worst; a set of references that spoke to a different narcissistic wound from the unfiltered racism (such as the content panel set up to rule on the 'anti-semitism' of the artworks) and furious condescension emanating from German memory politics, though the language of the art critic and the language of the state often converged – in large part by contesting the rightfulness of a claim to an avant-garde in content, if not in name. That liberal whiteness not only describes but owns the avant-garde – here the byword for political aesthetics – was the upshot of this unedifying psychodrama, and it will almost certainly not be the last.

Finally, another current dispute in the legacy of the avant-garde from a decolonial perspective is brewing in the relationship of Ukrainian and Russian cultural producers and activists to their shared and discrete histories. The notion of the Soviet avant-garde as a common reference point starts to buckle under the pressure of the ongoing Russian military aggression, and the imperialist cracks start to emerge in the agreement over what was a common revolutionary horizon. This horizon, or a future past, is located in a past that has begun to splinter, not as it did in the immediate post-Soviet era, but among people on the anti-authoritarian cultural left who had similar commitments to the unrealised revolutionary potentials of a historical experience that was assumed to have been in large part shared.

Other Sequences

The proposition of this text is the deceptively simple one that there must be a way of separating the claim on totality represented by the avant-garde from the parochial linearity of its concept of time. Or, to put it otherwise, to detach the transversality of the historical avant-garde's cultural and aesthetic politics – which in some cases, such as a revolutionary milieu, took on the dimensions that I've described elsewhere as 'infrastructural' – from the speciousness of a vanguard in an era without party or programme. By 'totality,' I am referring to capitalist existence as a 'concrete universal,' that is, a contradictory unity comprised of many particularities and overdetermined by the capitalist imperative to extract profit and subjugate labour and nature. The institutions of art have often served as consensus-building mechanisms in this totality, structurally and ideologically laundering this imperative and offering avenues of representation of alterity that remain notional on the whole so far as their own conditions of possibility are not at stake.

But in terms of the utility of the category of the avant-garde itself, a further problem comes up when, like 'artistic autonomy,' it is used not merely in the absence of the historical conditions in which it arise and persisted (mass society) but in the deliquiescence of the main category it defined itself *against*: modernism.[6] As already noted in the reference to Peter Osborne's discussion, the avant-garde was 'ahead' of modernism if modernism was the status quo, the ideology of a complacent

---

6   But see Chrysi Andriani Papaiannou: "The avant-garde is *at once a qualitative and a chronological category*. It is through focussing upon the mediation and the unresolved tension between qualitative and quantitative time, I contend, that we are best able to consider the chronopolitical complexities of the meaning of the idea of the avant-garde 'after modernism.'" Papaiannou, *Ahead of its Time: Historicity, Chronopolitics, and the Idea of the Avant-Garde after Modernism*, unpublished PhD thesis, University of Leeds, 2017.

bourgeois society; it was explicitly future-oriented, aiming to bring about the future as a rupture with the present, not wait for the next product line to emerge and exert its benign influence on social relations. When the future as a progressive category, explicitly as anything *but* a product line, has vanished from the contemporary vantage (with the 'contemporary' as the index of this), then the avant-garde as a substantive notion makes no sense at all. Progress, futurity, futurism – all have been lately tested and found non-performative, whether in the conventional or critical sense. So are there other political understandings of temporality which can help us approach this stagnation, this atomisation, differently than simply disputing a 'normativity' of productive time? Is there an understanding of time that departs from the concrete universal of the capitalist totality and can redeem the avant-garde's non-identity with it minus the simplifications of the avant-garde's hopes to transcend it? Are there, finally, a Marxist politics of time that can help us approach this whole question from angles which are not exhausted by the ethical and the historicist readings we've seen?

A departure point may be to understand in which sense temporality and spatiality are bourgeois categories, emerging from Enlightenment science and industry, guided by their concepts of efficiency and transparency. The pluralism of time is an important epistemic riposte, as can be seen in the work of decolonial thought; yet the epistemic critique may only be one layer of the critique of time as a lived, material dimension of capitalist social relations. The concept of time we're looking for is one that articulates totality as process, always contested and incomplete – a 'speculative totalization' rather than the 'total subsumption' that has featured heavily in much Western communist and critical theory over the past couple of decades. In a discussion of the category of the avant-garde, this needs to be accompanied by the distinction between the avant-garde as a reading of temporality (prescriptive) and the avant-garde as a periodizing category in Western art history (descriptive). Insofar as the former is used to yoke a certain reading of temporality to a proper form for the relationship between art and a revolutionary politics, it is a prescription that needs to be untangled.

To do this, we may wish to look to some recent interventions in Marxist theories of both time and temporality. Peter Osborne, whose work on the avant-garde and modernism as discrete notions of historical time in cultural and aesthetic politics has already been alluded to, writes, in terms that anticipate his later reading of the 'contemporary,' of the 'peculiar *de*-historicalizing temporality of capital, or capitalist sociality, which by and large constitutes – although it in no way exhausts – the temporality of the social for the vast majority of humankind today.'[7] This is the temporality that renewed calls for an analytic of the avant-garde hope to shape and infuse with determinate content, drawing a sharp line from the amorphousness of both a dominant contemporaneity *and* a dominant 'criticality' as the conditions for the unceasing production of globalised art. Osborne's diagnosis chimes with Moishe Postone's depiction of socially necessary abstract labour time as the generic form and 'norm' of capitalist modernity; what he calls 'the domination of people by time' is both historically specific and abstract, as abstract as the 'empty, homogeneous' time that acts as a measure, becoming an independent rather than a dependent variable, as it was when time was contingent on the

---

7   Peter Osborne, "Marx and the Philosophy of Time," *Radical Philosophy*, no. 147, 2008, 15-22; 16.

specific activity in question.[8] For both, the time of capital and modern historical temporality are dialectically inter-related, both on the structural level of capital being value-in-motion, that is, it can only be valorised in time, and in the experiential level where, post- the headlong rush of modernization, at least in the West, time seems to become evacuated and stand still, when it is not hurtling towards human and ecological disaster. On these accounts, an avant-garde would be impossible because there is nothing to get in front of; the expansive abstraction of capitalist time has subsumed all potentiality of an excessive, contingent or authentic creative life – these categories taken as immanent to the term 'avant-garde' - as it has 'normed' the whole of social life. However, another Marxist thinker of time and temporality, Massimiliano Tomba, proposes a significantly different take in his insistence on mixed and heterogeneous, 'geological' temporalities in capitalism. Such a reading opens up the totalization of abstract time over space and over history advanced by Postone, but also finds the generativity of struggle and openness to rupture in this heterogeneity which for Osborne represents the frozen conflict of globalised capitalist 'contemporaneity' – multiple times without a common denominator aside from their domination by the form of value. For Tomba, '[i]rregular sequences, aperiodic forms, unpredictable recurrences, fractal motifs, magnificent shapes of determinate complexity . . .' counter the 'absolutization of one historical temporality' achieved by many Marxist approaches to the geopolitics of time which lose sight of the mediations between the abstraction of the form of value and the distinctive historical and geographical experiences of it, what Tomba adroitly describes as the 'reciprocal implication of capitals with diffe-

---

8   Postone discusses the emergence of a uniform or abstract time which becomes a "compelling norm," "socially 'real' and 'meaningful'" Moishe Postone, *Time, Labor and Social Domination: A Reinterpretation of Marx's Critical Theory* (Cambridge: Cambridge University Press, 1993), 211-12.

rent organic compositions.' The expansion of capital creates frictions, some of which it successfully subsumes and turns to purposes of greater or new valorisation, and some of which present barriers, or even reorientations from other social forces. His insistence on considering capitalist time 'from the perspective of its historical temporalities and their friction, both among themselves and with other temporalities'[9] is notably useful not just for Marxist theory but also to art historical and art theoretical projects that work with the category of the avant-garde. In these terms, the category of the avant-garde is untenable, since its spatial and temporal relations are precisely those of 'one historical temporality,' with a front and a rear and a normative content. The correction of abstractly totalizing readings of capitalist temporality is, significantly, not just a matter of the keeping in view of mediation by concrete and historical particulars that is required for the careful researcher. Rather, it is at the very core of how capital works in actual time and space where the plurality of the times of capital comes in, namely, the difference between socially necessary labour time and abstract labour time, the problems in synchronizing recalcitrant labour – in and out of the waged workplace – to the capitalist time norm. This pluralism, this friction, this negativity of labour to abstract time, is perhaps closer to where we should be looking for resistance to the dominant (as well as to the acquiescent) that the category of the avant-garde applied to contemporary art production seeks. This would require additionally an acknowledgement that the grammar of ahead-behind, future-past, *avant-retardaire* relies on a temporal and spatial understanding which is not only linear, and thus long accused of being scientifically no less than morally 'incorrect,' but partaking fully in a historically and socially determined, class-bound, understanding of what we understand by 'time' and 'space' as preliminaries

---

9   Massimiliano Tomba, *Marx's Temporalities* (Leiden: Brill, 2012), 496-500.

of a subject-object relation whose felt primordiality occludes their bourgeois genealogy. First they were bourgeois categories, famously codified by Immanuel Kant as the conditions for all possible knowledge and all possible experience. Then they became 'categories of capital' used to 'organize human life and social relationships well beyond the intent and will of individual people,' as Tomba notes.[10] At the same time, we don't get anywhere with jettisoning these categories, nor a related category such as the 'avant-garde,' so long as we are living in a world where they apply. The avant-garde, to be sure, is a *critical* category, so doing away with it also means doing away with the critical charge it carries, which, as this essay has been proposing, should be retained but defined through a different set of concepts which do not reinforce the normativity – rather than the criticality – conveyed by the notion's proximity to the notions of time and space that organise the social relation it wants to challenge. Such an address to the 'rationality of the real' is basic to the dialectical approach, which seeks, in the field of conceptual no less than social contestation, '[c]ollisions proceeding from the very conditions of bourgeois society' which 'must be overcome by fighting, they cannot be reasoned out of existence.'[11] Time and space can also become dependent variables by means of artistic practice as it flows into social movements and processes of organizing, where the identity of the artist as the value-form of the field becomes redundant and

---

10   Ibid., 491.

11   Karl Marx, "The June Revolution" [1848], Karl Marx and Friedrich Engels, *Marx and Engels Collected Works*, Vol. 7. (New York: International Publishers), 144–149, quoted by Gavin Walker in "Nationalism and the National Question," Beverley Skeggs, Sara R. Farris, Alberto Toscano and Svenja Bromberg (eds.), *SAGE Handbook of Marxism*, 384.

individuality is re-configured.[12] What this amounts to, '[i]f we are to understand these terms as operating differentially rather than normatively,'[13] as Zakiyyah Iman Jackson writes in reference to gender and sexuality as categories applied to histories of slavery and antiblackness, then time and space need to operate precisely as categories under pressure from political process and the production of subjectivity in their midst –here including the distinct form of aesthetic practices - rather than co-ordinates for an especially radical subject 'ahead' of society whose trade name is 'artist.' Such a socially speculative approach to the temporality of aesthetic practices would thus erode and run counter to the speculative subject whose structure emulates that of the one of capitalist valorisation[14] which the adoption of a linear temporality of 'forward' and 'backward' cannot help but provide an alibi for.

It remains to be added that such a deconstruction of 'avant-garde' remains a partial fulfilment of the necessary task of overcoming its mystifications so long as art as specialised and class-bound field of activity is not addressed. Art as a key element of bourgeois temporality insofar as it's 'ahead' or 'elsewhere' or 'otherwise' as a structure of thought and practice. Dave Beech has written extensively, and with an admirable degree of historical-practical insight, how the emergence of the Western category of art was for several centuries the process

---

12   "When you participate, you're still an artist, but the things that you care about and produce, the productions that you make in that dimension, are completely different. You become anonymous. These dimensions can have their own time, speed, and value." Here, Cici Wu is reflecting on her involvement in the 2019-20 Hong Kong uprising. Cici Wu & Yong Soon Min, *After La Vida nueva* catalogue, Whitney Museum of American Art Independent Study Program, 2019-20.

13   "Saidiya Hartman by Zakiyyah Iman Jackson," *BOMB*, Winter 2023. Accessed at https://bombmagazine.org/articles/saidiya-hartman/

14   Marina Vishmidt, *Speculation as a Mode of Production: Forms of Value Subjectivity in Art and Capital* (Chicago: Haymarket, 2019).

of struggle between different factions about the relationship between the skillsets of 'handicraft' and those of the 'concept' as the distinguishing mark of an artist in its modern definition, with the gulf opening up between them similarly part of a protracted and nationally differentiated process of the formation of classes and the emergence of institutions of education, accreditation, and connoisseurship.[15] This is a narrative that complicates the received schema of the modernity of the modern artist as something chiefly secured by the consolidation of a market for art outside the patronage relations of church and nobility. The key element here for our theme, however, is that this account shows that the professionalisation of the artist as a 'specialist of non-specialism,' that is, as the possessor of an elite, and partially non-codifiable set of skills of complex cognition and aesthetic sensibility – as well as critical relation to their field, and, latterly to the field of cultural theory and developments in contemporary society – is the outcome of a class conflict which is never definitively done. The artist as a figure is 'ahead' in certain ways, but the artistic mode of production is also 'behind,' being mainly situated in a web of craft-scale, mercantile relations within capitalism, neither formally nor really subsumed – the exceptionality which lends it market value, but also breathing room from certain forms of exploitation. In a discussion of the chronopolitics of art today, Beech's account is useful in its focus on the historical and the institutional, and the struggles and debates that should be foregrounded to de-naturalize either accepted narratives or their repudiation by arguments that downplay those antagonisms in favour of ethical and individualised critiques that remain abstract, and thus re-naturalize the framework in which ethical and individualised critique makes sense. Such abstraction continues to pervade even more radical critiques that are

---

15   Dave Beech, *Art and Labour: On the Hostility to Handicraft, Aesthetic Labour, and the Politics of Work in Art* (Chicago: Haymarket, 2021).

tangentially connected, even at all, with proximate struggles in their field, not to speak of wider and more systemic contradictions and catastrophes. This is a principle that many contemporary platforms for institutional critique in the art field, as well as workers' organising, are taking into account in their shift to infrastructural and propositional paradigms, both of criticism and activity.[16]

Conclusion

This essay has been concerned to develop the argument that the *concept* of the avant-garde needs to be disambiguated in order to preserve the *function* of the avant-garde. Namely, the temporal dimension that inheres in its forward-facing structure does not just need to be reversed, as with the back-to-front Benjaminian angel of messianic time, but splintered and multiplied, to take into account the differential production of temporal forms by capital as lived form, which cannot be reconciled strategically or conceptually in a vanguard model of art or politics. The function, on the other hand, is to register and make tangible a mode of political salience for aesthetic practices, or, more concretely, a capacity to invoke or engage processes of revolutionary social transformation. It is thus important to sustain a volatile, negative dialectic between the necessity of complete transformation, of the unceasing damage and destruction of the capitalist social relation busy destroying us, and the concrete differences and contingencies that define the world to be thus transformed, which are experienced from the scale of subjectivity to the scale

---

16   "While each element of the bourgeois apparatus of art – studio, gallery, museum, art school, art magazine – has been subjected to radical critique and appears to be continually in crisis, the absence of a revolution in art's bourgeois mode of production is signalled by the reiteration of their negation rather than their replacement with a rival set of institutions or social relations." Ibid., 27, n1.

of ecosystems. The dimension of temporality is significant because it defines both experience and expectation, the frame of the possible and the possibility of a future – one that increasingly defines the present as something which may or may not persist, rather than a known quantity in the distance. Thus we can think of temporality as a 'concrete universal' in which the abstract and concrete are different and inextricable modalities. Christopher Arthur, for example, speaks of concrete universals in terms which lay out how the abstract and concrete are necessarily related when he discusses the ontology of capital: "The formal side may be treated purely theoretically w/o incurring charge of false abstraction, it is the logic of capital. That's only one aspect of the concrete universal. The move to concretion is necessary both for the system and its analysis. That's also where we talk about the reproduction of capital and social reproduction."[17] It is on this note that I would like to conclude. Social reproduction evokes both the ideas of reproduction of things as they are, but also the maintenance of the life of things, people, and relations so that they can survive into a future which itself depends on their agency, their collective planning, in Harney and Moten's terms. Lisa Baraitser's writing on 'maintenance time' is notable here.[18] She is interested in finding modes of political creativity in the diverse and contradictory ways in which time is experienced and that can collapse past and present in a non-reproductive, non-developmental way, temporalities that turn mourning into militancy, or even in activist practices of blocking, stoppage, and occupation. In other words, to see diverse temporalities and potentials in maintenance, in the time of care, and not just to see them as a biologized repetition, as in

---

17   Chris Arthur, *The Spectre of Capital: Idea and Reality* (Leiden: Brill, 2022), 271-272.

18   Lisa Baraitser, "Touching Time: Maintenance, Endurance, Care," Stephen Frosh (ed.), *Psychosocial Imaginaries: Perspectives on Temporality, Subjectivities and Activism* (London: Palgrave Macmillan, 2015), 21-47.

Hannah Arendt's notion of the home as timeless, as opposed to the public sphere, the proper site of politics.[19] That sustaining people, things, and relations over time is just as important to transformation, and just as creative as acts of rupture. But such a 're-valorisation' of maintenance does not exclude rupture so much as de-mystifies it. Perhaps in doing so it provides better resolution instruments for seeing it, as well as practicing it.

---

19   Hannah Arendt, *The Human Condition* (Chicago: University of Chicago Press, 1958), 30.

Soothing Conspiracies: Apology for an Unassuming Distributed Middle-Garde

Yves Citton

Some of us have lived many lives in many centuries before this one. Some of us have inhabited a multiplicity of worlds. We've done all this by talking with people, reading books, watching films, playing video games – all forms of being together, making love, partly in flesh, partly by proxy. Now we are here, doubting how many creatures and critters, heroes and zeroes, genies and ghosts make parts of this "we." And, honestly, we don't care. What matters is what we do – all of us – with all of us, for all of us.

What part of our common "we" could be called an *avant-garde?* What past avant-gardes continue to animate us? Who among us is about to mastermind an avant-garde about to come? We don't know. And honestly we don't care. What matters is what avant-gardes do and have done – all of them – with all of us for all of us.

Many of us have felt immersed in (loud or mute) avant-gardes. Many of us have read brilliant theories about the avant-gardes.[1] Many of these theories have been critical about the avant-gardes. Many of us are all the wiser about the traps and illusions of the avant-gardes. Many of us feel simultaneously immersed and distanced from them as a result. A contradictory

---

1   Olivier Quintyn, *Valences de l'avant-garde: essai sur l'avant-garde, l'art contemporain et l'institution* (Paris: Questions théoriques, 2015).

position. But, honestly, we don't care. What matters is what this ambivalence towards the avant-gardes helps us to do – all the same – with all of us, for all of us.

Those of us who experience this ambivalence as a puzzling mix of tireless hope and exhausted disarray may feel "in the middle" – rather than "in the break." Being in the middle takes us backwards, compared to forging ahead as an avant-garde. Not on the forefront of disruption, but in the ambivalence of routines: *in medias res* (where Wendy Hui Kyong Chun stressed a resonance with *media* and with *race*)[2]. Being in the middle may bring us closer to the undistinguished ranks of the multitudes. But it may also downgrade us to the shameful status of a "middle class" (Western? Global?). In any case, being in the middle tends to make us focus on present means rather than ultimate ends, on media rather than messages, on maintenance rather than on exploits, on common ways rather than unique arts. Being in the middle makes us rather dull. But, honestly, we don't care. What matters is what being in the middle may allow us to do – all differently – with all of us for all of us.

We, in the middle, may be dull, but we sincerely love and admire those who succeed by pushing themselves (and somehow remaining) in the break.[3] We truly love and admire them: we love and admire the truth they manage to distil from the middle of us. We are not envious of their strength, genius, and glory. We are inspired by them. We aspire to conspire with them. We breathe larger and truer breaths thanks to them. They matter: being in the break often comes with great dangers, and we are humbly grateful for their courage.

---

2   Wendy Hui Kyong Chun, *Programmed Visions: Software and Memory* (Cambridge, MA: MIT Press, 2011), 175-180.

3   Fred Moten, *In the Break: The Aesthetics of the Black Radical Tradition* (Minneapolis: University of Minnesota Press, 2003).

By breaking ground, they advance what happens in the middle – all the time – as a result of what they do in the break with all of us, for all of us.

From the middle of us comes something more humble. An apology rather than a manifesto or a claim. An apology for being a middle-garde rather than an avant-garde. An apology for being intermediaries rather than discoverers or inventors. An apology for being distributors and distributed rather than creators and concentrated. An apology for being unassuming when audacious assertions (loud and clear) and daring actions (bold and decisive) are urgently needed. An apology for being caught – most of us – between paralyzing gestures of Great Refusal and incoming promises of Great Upheaval.

Our apology could sound like this...

We Love You, Elvin, Tony, Ed, Famoudou, Vinnie, Gerry, Hamid, Susie, Jim & Tyshawn

How do we, in the middle, experience the avant-garde as a living force within and among us? By listening to drummers like Elvin Jones, Tony Williams, Ed Blackwell, Famoudou Don Moye, Vinnie Colaiuta, Hamid Drake, Gerry Hemingway, Susie Ibarra, Jim Black or Tyshawn Sorey. Not only because, with their magic sticks, they beat the shit out of our daily routines. Not only because they pulse and impulse into our bodies a rhythmicity that accompanies and swings us days, weeks, years after we've heard them play. Not only because they work – work it out! – from within the break, driving the beat always a little ahead of itself, pushing it forward, pushing us forward, ahead of our selves, beyond our tempo, beyond our time, just enough to embody and incorporate a feel of the future which will, in return, make our present more urgent, more urging to short-circuit what is still dragging us back.

This is all enormous, awesome and priceless, this tireless work they accomplish from their drum seat with their bare hands – all of them, Elvin, Tony, Ed, Famoudou, Vinnie, Gerry, Hamid, Susie, Jim & Tyshawn. This is the work of the avant-garde at its highest – Free Jazz, the New Thing, Great Black Music, Harmolodics, Creative Music, Avant-Jazz.

But contrary to other heroes of the avant-gardes, drummers push us forward from the back of the stage, from the middle of the band. They support the soloists from the background position of the rhythm section. Their drum solos can be astonishing, but the top of their art shines in the form of sustained interactions, joint improvisations – from the middle of an ensemble. They are never alone at the top, they always bring others with them, they elevate others to the top of their capacity (and sometimes beyond), they levitate them (and us along the way). Elvin Jones & John Coltrane & McCoy Tyner, Tony Williams & Miles Davis & Wayne Shorter, Ed Blackwell & Ornette Coleman & Don Cherry, Famoudou Don Moye & Lester Bowie & Joseph Jarman & Roscoe Mitchell & Malachi Favors, Vinnie Colaiuta & Frank Zappa, Gerry Hemingway & Anthony Braxton & Marilyn Crispell & Mark Dresser, Hamid Drake & William Parker & Ken Vandermark, Susie Ibarra & David S. Ware, Jim Black & Tim Berne, Tyshawn Sorey & Steve Lehman & Vijay Iyer.

Drummers challenge our heroic view of the avant-garde because they perform supporting acts. Their assigned role is one of maintenance: keep the beat, maintain the pace, watch the time. On the face of it, they don't express themselves: they work (hard): they sweat, they labor – for the band, for the ensemble, for the assembly. They drive from the back seat, never on their own, never for their own sake, but always for their fellow-musicians – with all of them for all of them.

Drummers unite. Drummers expand. Their back-seat driving is not contained within the limits of the stage. Their syncopations push the audience's bodies to bend forward or backwards, to oscillate in pace with the bass drum. Their meanderings around the beat, their beating around the bush of metronomic time destabilize us. They make us briefly lose our balance, until they catch us before we fall, with a slight delay on the snare drum. Even years after their actual performance and sweat, their recordings manage to have us hold our breath, move our feet, shake our head. We are alone at home, in a waiting room, on the bus, headphones on, and they still move our body, they still animate our minds, they still push us forward with their syncopated beat – in time and through time – with all of us, for all of us.

But if some of us would like to portray drummers as emblems of the middle-garde, it is also, and perhaps mostly, because drummers *play* the drums. They don't just perform: they play. Always in playful mood. Even when the hour is dark and the circumstances dreadful (Elvin & John playing *Alabama*). They are fully present – more intensely present than we will ever be "in real life" – and yet, they know and we know that they are "on a stage." Playing. A little beside themselves. Famoudou Don Moye paints his face. Hamid Drake wears colorful clothes. They are no mere agents, they are actors. Their work is as serious as your life, but they never take themselves too seriously. They smile and they laugh (about it all). One foot inside, one foot outside (the beat, the play, the game, the role). They make us laugh in disbelief ("How could he do *that*?!") and smile in complicity ("Well done!") – with all of us for all of us.

As their play is by essence collective, they are master improvisers. Some of the avant-gardes may have posed as programmers: they write ahead of time (in a manifesto) what others or themselves will later be called to enact (along the guidelines established in the manifesto). Drummers may play previously written compositions of course – we love you, Ornette Coleman, Cecil Taylor, Antony Braxton, Henry Threadgill, Frank Zappa, Tim Berne, Ken Vandermark, Mary Halvorson. But drummers always readjust their touch on the skin of their drums according to the singular moment of interaction with other band members – with all of them for all of them.

Middle-gardes are bound to improvise because we are never fully ahead of our times, always in-between what we think we know about the future and what we don't know about the present. One foot inside, one foot outside. We are bound to "improvise" because nobody has "provided us with" the proper knowledge on what is to be done. The discovery of what we wanted in the first place always comes along the way, in a necessarily collective movement where it is crucial to stay in touch with all of us for all of us – *i.e.*, to play a game of collective improvisation – from the subcutaneous to the planetary in an ecopolitics of dancing.[4]

In other words, improvisers may be strategists and (fugitive) planners, but they are first and foremost *conspirers*: they learn (and teach) how to *breathe together*, at the same pace or alternatively, but within the same air, the same atmosphere, the same milieu. Drummers drive conspiracies, where musicians and audiences share an upbeat complicity[5].

---

4   Emma Bigé, *Mouvementements. Ecopolitiques de la dance* (Paris: La Découverte, 2023).

5   Valentina Desideri and Stefano Harney, "A conspiracy without a plot," Jean-Paul Martinon and Irit Rogoff (eds.), *The Curatorial: A Philosophy of Curating* (London: Bloomsbury, 2013), 125-136.

Gardeners of the Middle

Do great drummers make great heroes of the revolution? Do we really want a revolution? Do we really need heroes? True avant-gardes would not hesitate to say yes. We have our doubts. Do we identify the middle-garde with a middle ground, equally wary about all forms of extremism? We have our doubts. Are we committed to bring down capitalism, as it becomes clearer and clearer every day that its extractivist dynamics are wrecking our communities and ravaging our habitats? We are. Do we believe a revolution is realizable and desirable way to bring it down? We have our doubts.

Some of us suspect that the more one talks about agency, the less one acts. We know people come together. By coming together, they can deeply alter political institutions. And political institutions need to be deeply altered. But we suspect that, in order for such alterations to produce satisfactory outcome, they need to brew in the middle. They usually emerge from the margins and the breaks, but they come together in and from the middle. From the middle, that we form by coming together.

Forming a middle, also known as a milieu, is no easy task. It requires effort, and great care. Capitalism must be dismantled because it undermines our living milieus – in the literal sense of that verb: its extractivism mines and exhausts, undoes and ruins the socio-ecological ground on which we live and from which it profits. In order to repel its extractivism, one needs to maintain, nourish, and strengthen the milieu we form by coming together, even if capitalism ultimately profits from this milieu it undermines and we sustain. We have no choice because this milieu – our neighborhood, our town, our bioregion, planet Earth – is the only we will ever have to live on. There is no planet B. This much we know.

We are a middle-garde because we see ourselves as wardens and gardeners of this milieu from and within which we live. Wherever we may be, this comes first: caring over our common milieu, with all of us, for all of us.

And that may be why, as middle-gardeners, we don't make very effective political and revolutionary agents. Revolutionary politics needs enemies – (groups of) individuals that are portrayed as separated from all of us. "Them." Political agency needs "them." Do we need political agency? Some of us have doubts.

Middle Class Conservationism

As oppressed people, we do not need to look for enemies, to make "them" up. We suffer from "them" and we often have good reasons to hate "them." Our socio-environmental milieu, our garden, our loved ones have been damaged, ruined, amputated, killed by capitalism and its colonial agents. So politics should come naturally, generously endowed with hate against "them." And revolutions should have blasted away capitalism long ago.

But they haven't (so far). So we have our doubts about the whole "them or us" scheme that is currently identified with revolutionary politics.

What if a good number among us who are oppressed by capitalism were also somewhat driven by and towards it? What if a good number of us – not all, for sure – felt somewhat caught in the middle, between hate and distraction. Not love, for sure. Not appeal either. Not even attraction. Distraction sounds as close as possible to what it is. And one rarely hates those who distract us. One may even like being occasionally distracted and entertained. Taken away from where we are. A little distanced from those to whom we may feel excessively attached.

Not too close, not too tightly knit with what we are. A little removed. Not fully here, not totally there. In between the inside and the outside. Somewhere in the middle. Not in a "neutral" position, as if one could escape conflicts. But in a *neutrition* attitude, which metabolizes our inseparation by finding nutrition in tensions, rather than rest in neutralized peace.[6]

What if capitalism contributed to emancipate us from the here and now? What if we were its accomplices in this distraction? What if we liked and desired it, as much as we hate and resent it? We may hate "them" for what capitalism leads them to do to us. But some of us can't help feeling that we are also a part of what capitalism do to us, including the very oppression from which we suffer. And we don't want to hate ourselves for what capitalism has us do to our selves.

So rather than calling out enemies in "them," we tend to feel a part of "them" in "ourselves." Which makes us unreliable political agents and untrustworthy revolutionaries. Which makes it perfectly understandable for real revolutionaries – those who struggle in the break, those identified with the avant-garde we love and admire – to consider us with some amount of contempt.

Isn't our middle-garde attitude typical of the wishy-washiness of all middle classes? Call us softies. Uncommitted. We are the ones who undo revolutions, when revolutions start dangerously to undo the ruling order. We dodge taking side. We are neither here nor there. Neither (fully) for, nor (really) against. One foot inside, one foot outside. We keep our doubts when full commitment is required by the emergency. Instead of forging ahead full force, screaming our lungs out to repel our anxieties and to

---

6   Lila Braunschweig, *Neutriser. Émancipations(s) par le neutre* (Paris: Les Liens qui Libèrent, 2021) and Dominique Quessada, *L'inséparé. Essai sur un monde sans autres* (Paris: PUF, 2013).

panic our enemies, we consider our options. We keep hoping for negotiations. Some of us even hedge their bets.

We are middle-men, middle-women, afraid of being caught in the middle in case of conflicts. So we avoid antagonism, at almost any cost. Of course, we know about the General Antagonism, the one which structures all unequal and unjust societies. Far from ignoring it, we see it everywhere. We fear it everywhere, because we know it can always spiral down into civil war. Avant-gardes strive to trigger revolutions. Middle-gardes strive to prevent civil wars.

We side with the people who loathe taking side because they know they will end up caught in the middle. Revolutionaries call us cowards, or opportunists. Or worse: pacifists. But we are not so much afraid of dying as we are afraid of damaging the relational milieu with which we so fully, so desperately identify. We don't fight (on battlefields), we conspire (in back alleys). Actively maintaining relationships of common breath and of shared air matters more to us than winning a war. That's why we are seen as conservatives, conservationists. Surely, nothing could be further removed from the revolutionary avant-garde than our conservationist middle-garde conspiracy. All apologies.

The Great Upheaval and the Terrestrial Pivot

And yet... Something, deep inside, in the middle of us, tells us that the middle-garde may be the surprising avant-garde of tomorrow's worlds. For the times, and the gardes, have been changing. The 20th century is over. So perhaps its avant-gardes. Calls for the Great Revolution have given way to postures of Great Refusal. But these, we suspect, will be washed away by the Great Upheaval.

This Great Upheaval was well described by Congolese writer Sony Labou Tansi as early as 1990, when he warned us about an incoming "war of the worlds, the one that will henceforth oppose the center of the wealthy world to its various peripheries, near or far, unless the forces of interplanetary solidarity prevail over all the logics of enslavement": "the emergence of a common destiny for all humans (ecology, raw materials seen in the light of the just price)" demands to "institute solidarity as a new golden rule of the world game, next to the already very fragile notion of the sovereign right to power."[7]

(*From the middle of us, a voice asks*: hasn't this "Great Upheaval" already taken place, from the moment the Europeans started ravaging the places and populations they conquered? Aren't we *already* in a state of civil war? Good questions! Sony Labou Tansi *both* unveiled the war *already* waged against African people *and* warned us about the (incoming, worsening) war of the worlds in a renewed context of "interplanetary solidarity." Similarly, the general antagonism makes it both impossible for us in the middle (class) to say "we," and impossible not to identify with the mixed bunch and motley crew inhabiting "our" common milieu.) In an age of extreme environmental destruction, the middle ground will be the only inhabitable one, on a planetary as well as on a local scale. Our political compass is pivoting by a 90° turn (clockwise). The old South is the new West: our vanguard comes from Africa (Great Black Music). The old North will be the new East: not so much China's leadership, as the melting of the Arctic under the heat of the rising sun. Conquest and productive growth will have to give way to maintenance and reproductive wisdom. Avant-garde warriors to middle-garde care-workers.

---

7   Sony Labout Tansi, "Lettre aux intellocrates de la médiocratie parlementaire" [1990], *Encre, sueur, salive et sang* (Paris: Seuil, 2015), 145-146.

In Bruno Latour's vocabulary: the past centuries organized politics around a "modernizing frontier" which opposed progressives bound to the Global attractor of transnational logistics, to reactionaries bound to the Local attractor of inherited traditions; the "New Climate Regime" of the Anthropocene opposes reactionaries bound to an "Out-of-This-World" attractor, desperately claiming to Make America (or your favorite sovereign nation) Great Again, to progressives bound towards a Terrestrial attractor whose main challenge is to provide earthly creatures with an inhabitable milieu. "Dramatizing somewhat extravagantly, let us call it a conflict between modern humans who believe they are alone in the Holocene, in flight toward the Global or in exodus toward the Local, and the terrestrials who know they are in the Anthropocene and who seek to cohabit with other terrestrials under the authority of a power that as yet lacks any political institution. And that war, at once civic and moral, divides each of us from within."[8]

We, in the middle-garde, understand that Sony Labou Tansi's "war of the worlds" is not a future threat, but a present reality of globalization inherited from the colonial past. This war has killed and maimed millions of people, mostly in the South. Not only is it still raging on, but it is pivoting, in a 90° turn which Achille Mbembe has described as a becoming-black (*devenir-nègre*) of middle-class populations all across the world.[9]

This ongoing aggression of capitalist colonization is not only an economic and political conquest. It is also a war, at once civic and moral, which divides each of us from within. It assaults and splits us from the middle. And it can only be counter-attacked from the middle – by means of de-escalation.

---

8   Bruno Latour, *Down to Earth* (Cambridge: Polity Press, 2018), 90.

9   Achille Mbembe, *Critique of Black Reason* (Durham: Duke University Press, 2017).

Such is the 90° pivot called forth by the incoming Great Upheaval: from modern humans to terrestrials, from Whiteland to becoming-black, from warmongers to de-escalators. From extremizing avant-gardes to soothing middle-gardes? In Mierle Laderman Ukeles' 1969 vocabulary, from development to maintenance: "The Death Instinct: separation, individuality, Avant-Garde par excellence; to follow one's path to death – do your own thing, dynamic change. / The Life Instinct: unification, the eternal return, the perpetuation and MAINTENANCE of the species, survival systems and operations, equilibrium. / Two basic systems: Development and Maintenance. The sourball of every revolution: after the revolution, who's going to pick up the garbage on Monday morning?"[10]

Self-Defeating Capitalism from its Middle

Not so fast!… All of this soft talk about conflict dodging, supposedly bound to Earth, is more probably bound to let capitalism rule in peace. This soothing and pacifying middle-garde may indeed prevent conflict – but at the price of filling everybody's mouth with soothers and pacifiers. A billion of people in China are becoming middle-class over a couple of generations, selling their free thought for comfort and commodities (so we're told). The Middle Empire is proudly carrying the torch of extractivist oppressive self-destruction, in a global pivot abundantly commented upon by the Obama administration.

Should we simply follow along? "Maintain" capitalism? Our mouth shut around pacifiers, frozen by the fear of conflict? Play the ultimate suckers?

---

10   Mierle Laderman Ukeles, "Maintenance Art Manifesto. Proposal for an Exhibition: CARE," 1969. See also Jérôme Denis and David Pontille, *Le soin des choses. Politiques de la maintenance* (Paris: La Découverte, 2022).

Open confrontation or resigned submission, resistance or collaboration, freedom or death: many among us suspect such binary questions miss the point. If the point could be made – what we have is not so much a constellation of points as an entanglement of lines – it could go somewhat like this:

Capitalism == Extractivism + Sovereignism + Colonialism + Patriarchy + Speculation

As we all know, colonialism did not stop around the middle of the 20th century. It has pursued its course under the new clothes of globalization. But it has altered its mode of organization and somewhat weakened its mode of domination. Anticolonial struggles have won national independence. Decolonial activism is slowly but constantly eroding colonial mindsets. While assessing the many contradictions of where we are *After the Great Refusal*, Mikkel Bolt Rasmussen ask the question: *Have we already won?*[11] Not yet, surely. If it is not reduced to a metaphor, decolonization still has a long way to go.[12] And, like the anticolonial struggles, it bears mostly on those who are in the break. But the undoing of colonialism may be in the (slow) process of expanding to the middle. So let us anticipate:

Capitalism – Colonialism == Extractivism + Sovereignism + Patriarchy + Speculation

From contraception to obtaining the right to vote, from the recognition of domestic labor to *#MeToo*, from gay rights to the trans movement, the last hundred years have done more than any other period in modern history to undo patriarchy. More to the point: ecofeminism can be seen as the truest form

---

11   Mikkel Bolt Rasmussen, *After the Great Refusal: Essays on Contemporary Art, Its Contradictions and Difficulties* (London: Zero Books, 2018), 119.

12   Eve Tuck and K. Wayne Yang, "Decolonization is not a metaphor," *Decolonization: Indigeneity, Education & Society*, vol. 1, no. 1, 2012, 1–40.

of politics by the milieu, with the emphasis it puts on caring for the webs of people, things and powers.[13] *Have we already won?* Not fully, of course. Because patriarchy is a vicious and relentless beast, because our (dis)connected forms of life mass-produce incels, because backlashes locally succeed. But here more than anywhere else, we have already come a long way. So let us look forward:

Capitalism – Colonialism – Patriarchy == Extractivism + Sovereignism + Speculation

Extractivism is a hard one to expel from capitalism. We clearly have not won that one. A good number of us in the middle still rely on it. Extractivism is that war, at once civic and moral, at once economic and political, which divides each of us from within. As such, it can't be won. It is simultaneously what feeds us and what kills us – this indiscriminating "us" being one of "our" main obstacles. Extractivism can't be defeated (from the outside). It needs to be *dismantled* (from the middle).[14]

The infrastructures we have built to fulfill our needs (and exacerbate our desires) generate countless collateral damages – which, we realize, are not "collateral" at all (mere externalities), but dramatically central to our ecocidal modes of production. They unleash "feral" effects from the very core of our "civilization."[15] An ecology of dismantlement cannot simply vanquish such feral effect, crush them down, eradicate them, blow them out of existence. All of our feral technologies follow more or

---

13 Starhawk, *Webs of Power: Notes from the Global Uprising* (Philadelphia: New Society, 2003).

14 Alexandre Monnin, Diego Landivar and Emmanuel Bonnet, *Héritage et fermeture: une écologie du démantèlement* (Paris: Divergences, 2021).

15 Anna Tsing et al., *Feral Atlas*, https://feralatlas.org/ (a Stanford Digital Project, 2020).

less the model of our nuclear power plants: the worst thing would be to annihilate them, to bomb them, to forget about them and look away. As Timothy Morton warned us, there is no "away" to throw such things away.[16] Like plastic waste, like climate change, they are awfully sticky: we are stuck with them – all of us, rich (less painfully) and poor (more cruelly).

Dismantling can't be an act of war. It is a practice of care. It is based upon the acknowledgement of our shared vulnerability, rather than upon the boasting of our sovereign capacity.[17] It does not fit with the military conception of the avant-garde. It is an art of the middle – an art of repair, cooperation, maintenance, listening, soothing. Can we overcome extractivism? Not so much by confronting it, not so much by shaming each other for the part we take in it, but rather by carefully dismantling it. Slowly, humbly, progressively – even if time is awfully short. So let's accelerate:

Capitalism – Colonialism – Patriarchy – Extractivism == Sovereignism + Speculation

As we also know, sovereignism is on the rise. The hopes of the alter-globalization movements have been strangled by the clamp of global logistics and of reactionary nationalism. Not only are "patriotic" parties gaining ground across many countries, rich and poor, but they openly spread across the whole political spectrum, from the traditional xenophobic far-right (Italy) to social democrats (Denmark) to significant currents of the labor parties (France). As Mikkel Bolt Rasmussen convincingly argued, "late capitalist fascism" is not to be seen as a threat to democracy, from the part of

---

16   Timothy Morton, *Hyperobjects. Philosophy and Ecology after the End of the World* (Minneapolis: University of Minnesota Press, 2013).

17   Joan Tronto, *Moral Boundaries: A Political Argument for an Ethic of Care* (London: Routledge, 1993).

the far-right: it is an inherent tendency of our mediarchical democracies.[18] It comes from the middle of us, in its long-lasting attempt to take the authoritative center for the living milieu. It will have to be defeated in the years and decades ahead, if we are to prevent (a worsening of) the "war of the worlds" by pragmatically acknowledging "the emergence of a common destiny for all humans (ecology, raw materials seen in the light of the just price)."

We deluded ourselves into fantasizing various forms of sovereignty, mostly based upon the exploitation, oppression and repression of our shared incompleteness.[19] The turning point may still be ahead of us. The pivot. No longer (sovereign) freedom or death. No longer them or us. Antagonism is part of the problem, not the solution. Or rather: partial antagonisms (between sovereign claims) are our only true enemy in our common struggle against the general antagonism.

Can we win against sovereignism? Precisely not. Because winning is in itself a sovereign claim. Victory too needs to be dismantled in its ferality. To do so, we need another culture of collective action, wary of the martial tones of the avant-gardes – a culture of the middle-gardes. Let's precipitate the pivot:

Capitalism – Colonialism – Patriarchy – Extractivism – Sovereignism == Speculation

---

18   Mikkel Bolt Rasmussen, *Late Capitalist Fascism* (Cambridge: Polity, 2022); Yves Citton, *Mediarchy* (Cambridge: Polity, 2019).

19   Stefano Harney and Fred Moten, *All Incomplete* (Wivenhoe: Minor Compositions, 2021).

Breathing Conspiracies for Speculative Futures

And so we're left with speculation – repeatedly denounced as a form of conspiracy. We have not won yet – far from it, of course. But capitalism seems in the process of coming undone from its middle. What remains of its "essence"? The private ownership of the means of production, Marx told us one and a half century ago (not so long, in anthropological times). The antagonism between the capitalist class (extractors of value) and the working class (deprived of the wealth it produces). No doubt, this scheme continues to structure industrial capitalism – and capitalism is industrial in its essence, from the Caribbean plantation until today's Chinese factories. But what about finance capitalism – and capitalism has been financial since its origins, from Genovese banks in the Renaissance until today's high-speed trading?

The capitalist class can accurately be identified with the 1%. With those portfolio holders currently in position to control (trade, sell, close) half of our common registered wealth. Finance is the technique of extraction of this half in favor of the 1%. Granted. But what about "the middle classes"? When they/we are (un)lucky enough to count on pension funds to provide for retirement, when they/we manage to put away some savings, when they/we take on debt to pursue studies, buy an apartment or launch a company, they/we become entangled/strangled with financial capitalism – a part of the problem, a cog in the extractivist machine.

Beyond the actual holding of debts or assets, Randy Martin has showed how the financialization of everyday life had permeated our existential experiences, our mental representations and our daily habits.[20] Finance is the extended and proliferating empire of the middle-men (more rarely middle-women). Its breath penetrates everywhere, inspires everyone, transpires in everything: its ubiquitous conspiracy is the living milieu of late (deadly or already-dead?) capitalism. Being in the middle makes finance structurally unstable. It bubbles and busts. More interestingly, it constantly inverts its flows. Up and down. Back and forth. Michel Feher has suggested this fundamental instability could be turned around against those who currently profit from it: once the debt is big enough, the debtor class can become an "investee" class, collectively too big to fail.[21] Investors don't want to lose their capital: they rely and depend upon the capacity of the investees to pay (some of) it back. And some of it may not be the total sum of it. The difference between the sum and the some is what finance attempts to anticipate, day in, day out – always in the middle.

(*From the middle of us, another voice asks*: doesn't the sweet dream of a Debtors' International omit the inherent tendency of the capitalist mode of production, which, from the Plantation on, was not a mode of (sustainable) reproduction, but of (self-proclaimed creative) destruction? It only raises future promises in order to loot present wealth.)

Traditionally, middle-men negotiate. But, mostly, finance *speculates*. Negotiations take place on the level of exchanges: when one buys a carpet or a second-hand motorcycle. Finance is something else. It takes place on a higher level of abstraction, on a larger scale of extraction. It does not trade things, commodities, but derivatives. Not directly values and prices, but second-level

---

20   Randy Martin, *The Financialization of Daily Life* (Philadelphia: Temple University Press, 2002).

21   Michel Feher, *Rated Agency: Investee Politics in a Speculative Age* (New York: Zone Books, 2018).

bets about future prices. As Elie Ayache cleverly suggested, finance does not negotiate anything with anyone: finance *writes*.[22] It writes off but, mostly, it writes prices. In almost the same fashion as a novelist writes a sentence of her novel.

The sentence does not preexist its writing (even if, obviously, the world in which the novelist writes her sentence preexists and conditions her writing). The writing of the sentence does not take place in advance of its time (like an avant-garde pretends to be). It cannot be probabilistically guessed on the basis of the past data (no matter how big or how powerfully computated these data happen to be). The writing of the sentence in a novel, as well as the writing of the price of a derivative, take place in the middle of the present. By attempting to view and anticipate the future, it partially writes – on and off – the future, but always in the present. In real time. This operation of writing in real time is what we commonly call *speculation*. (Oddly enough, it overlaps with what call *improvisation*.)

What if speculation was what we are left with once capitalism has been hollowed out of its extractivism, sovereignism, colonialism, patriarchy? Would we still have to consider it our enemy? Once we are left with speculation, what is left of speculation? Could it be a speculation from the Left? Or a futuristic improvisation from the middle? A drummers' conspiracy?

Over the past years, speculation has been trendy in various fields, a long way from finance, in philosophy and in design[23]. Branded as a technology of the future, it has sided with accelerationist avant-gardes – sometimes carried forth with soothsayers' postures. With more humility, Aris

---

22   Elie Ayache, *The Blank Swann: The End of Probability* (London: Wiley, 2010).

23   Anthony Dunne and Fiona Raby, *Speculative Everything* (Cambridge, MA: MIT Press, 2013).

Komporozos-Athanasiou's recent book portrays speculative communities as wandering souls in search of soothing reassurance in a radically uncertain world – an attitude more in tune with improvisational middle-gardes.[24]

We speculate (and improvise), first and foremost, because we know we don't know. But because we know we don't know, we brace ourselves and each other to jump-start desirable futures, and dodge unnecessary confrontations in the present. We wear yellow vests and occupy suburban roundabouts to fend off social injustice and greenwashing. We book tickets at a Trump rally we never meant to attend for the fun of seeing him speak in an empty stadium. We do speculate about possible futures in a world of uncertainty, but we mostly improvise in the present – with all of us, for all of us.

Is this speculative art? Or a middle-of-the-road art of speculation? Are we speculators? Of course not. Are we artists? Who knows? We are collective improvisers.[25] We assemble, online and on site, on public squares, in festivals and concert halls.[26] We stick together. We touch skins. We caress symbols. We gamble. We play. As do Elvin, Tony, Ed, Famoudou, Vinnie, Gerry, Hamid, Susie, Jim & Tyshawn, with their magic sticks, touching skins, caressing cymbals.

Ours is an art of *conspiracy*: breathing-together is both a premise (we are alive, therefore we breathe) and a goal (we must maintain a breathable living milieu). Drummers of the world,

---

24   Aris Komporozos-Athanasiou, *Speculative Communities: Living with Uncertainty in a Financialized World* (Chicago: University of Chicago Press, 2022).

25   George E. Lewis and Benjamin Piekut (eds.), *The Oxford Handbook of Critical Improvisation Studies* (Oxford: Oxford University Press, 2013).

26   Jonas Staal, "Assemblism," *e-flux journal*, no. 80, 2017, https://www.e-flux.com/journal/80/100465/assemblism/

we're uniting – breathing together in tune and in sync (insepa-rably synchronization and syncopation).

(*From the middle of us, yet another voice asks*: Can you beat capitalism with drumsticks? Probably Not. But then again: we're not so sure.)

It is true that, beside speculating and improvising, our con-spiracies need organizing – and we have a long way to scale, from jazz ensembles to planetary mobilizations.[27] But middle-gardes don't dream of beating anyone or anything in power or size. They need a driving pulse welcoming us to breathe together. We need to pace a common polyrhythm for a co-ha-bitable world. A middle world of soothing conspiracies.

---

27   Geert Lovink and Ned Rossiter, *Organization after Social Media* (Colchester: Minor Compositions, 2018).

Notes on Planetary Strategy: Metabolic Realism for Commoners

Gene Ray

The planetary meltdown initiated and driven by capitalism has brought modernist politics to its breaking point.[1] Compounding social and ecological crises have exposed problems of societal metabolism for which state and capital have no solution: the economic growth imperative and its world cannot be sustained without catastrophic damage to the biosphere. The failing squared circle of green growth is revealed to be a vicious downward spiral, spinning toward a hothouse earth and mass extinction. As evidence mounts that the 500-year project of capitalist modernity is reaching its limits, the global ruling classes have doubled down: the problem of societal metabolism and its economic driver is disavowed and will not be discussed.

The disavowal is spun and hustled by new weapons of mass distraction: the partial decarbonization of the "green energy transition" and promised magical rescue by much-hyped but

---

1   I thank Anna Papaeti, Mikkel Bolt Rasmussen, George Sotiropoulos and the comrades of Retort for their responses to these propositions. Parts of this essay are excerpted, with modifications for this context, from *After the Holocene: Planetary Politics for Commoners* (Brooklyn: Autonomedia, forthcoming). In this essay, I reconsider the problem of strategy, a main point at issue in leftwing political vanguardism, in light of the emerging planetary conjuncture. For my earlier discussions of the politics of artistic avant-gardes, in relation to anti-systemic movements and struggles, see Ray, "Toward a Critical Art Theory," in *Art and Contemporary Critical Practice: Reinventing Institutional Critique*, eds. Gerald Raunig and Gene Ray (London: MayFly Books, 2009), 79-91; and "Avant-Gardes as Anti-Capitalist Vector," *Third Text*, vol. 21, no. 3, 2007, 241-255.

still nonexistent new technologies. Again, the message echoes: there is no alternative, business-as-usual is the source of all prosperity and all security. And besides, even if there are alternatives, capitalist modernity is deemed impervious to political change due to "technological lock-in" and "socio-economic inertia."[2]

This does not mean the ruling classes are climate deniers. Having absorbed and "discounted" the findings of Earth System Science, they are wagering on their own capacity to adapt, survive, and dominate others as the planet burns and the seas rise. They are trusting that technology, innovation and above all security agencies (plus backdoor escape fantasies to New Zealand or Mars) will make the climate risks acceptable – to them. They fully understand that the reduction and deceleration of the growth machines would mean the end of capitalism and their class power. So, they have no choice but to carry on: everything else appears to be more dangerous. Since they have no alternative, they need to convince the rest of us that we don't either.

The disavowal and intransigence of capitalists and national security technocrats translates into intensified social antagonisms and accelerating ecological catastrophe: more death and violence, more ecocide, more border walls and exclusions, more austerity, surveillance and repression. Dissenters who defend the biosphere will from now on be treated as terrorists. But the high costs of systemic reproduction, now tasked with sustaining the unsustainable, are becoming intolerable: all that is left of global governance is the globalized crisis of legitimacy.

---

2   For a critical social sciences description of how capitalist economic logics result in "technological lock-in" and "socio-economic inertia, see Ulrich Brand, Barbara Muraca, Éric Pineault, et al., "From Planetary to Social Boundaries: An Argument for Collectively Defined Self-Limitation," *Sustainability: Science, Practice and Policy*, vol. 17, no. 1, 2021, 265-292.

Electoral democracy, corrupted to farce and goaded by misinformation and cyberwar campaigns, now gives birth to new fascisms: the ethno-nationalist barkers of panic politics stoke resentments and promise to make the nation great again. This is the de facto formula of planetary disavowal in the US (even under Biden), but also in Russia, China, and India. The real choices today belong to the commoners: to refuse this disavowal and organize to act accordingly.

This new conjuncture corresponds with waning US influence and the rapid rise of China. The much-discussed challenge to the so-called "rules-based international order" (an order Made in the USA, meaning that the US reserved the right to make the rules and also decide the exceptions to them) is an euphemism for a new round of intensified inter-imperialist competition. This time around, the key points of conflict will be the supply chains not just for fossil fuels but for the critical minerals and computer chips required for lithium-ion batteries, smartphones, AI, and weapons systems.[3]

The war in Ukraine opens a front in Europe, but the next fronts and flashpoints are easily identified: Africa (for the cobalt, coltan, and rare earths), Chile and the Andes (for the lithium), Indonesia and the Philippines (for the nickel), and Taiwan (for

---

3   The best place to read the climate imperialist mind debating itself is the website of *Foreign Affairs*, a favored house organ of the US foreign policy and national security establishment. There, day by day, hawks and doves, realists and legalists, globalists and post-globalists thrash out the implications of planetary "polycrisis" for US power and its international order. *Foreign Affairs*, famously read by Lenin, is published by the Council on Foreign Relations, one of the oldest "non-partisan" think-tanks.

the semiconductor chips).[4] Shifting much of the global energy system to so-called clean electricity and batteries will turn large parts of the global South into toxic open pit mines that will be festering wounds of environmental injustice, labor abuses, and bombed-out ecologies.[5] Once again, the North will try to sustain its advantages on the backs of the South.

The imminent drift of this climate imperialism is toward climate fascism and a third world war. Rivalries are being militarized, and active wars, such as Ukraine, are escalating at an alarming rate. Almost daily, voices from the national security complexes are issuing provocations and even hazarding predictions about when the war between the US and China will break out in the South China Sea.[6] Such a war would pull all the other nations in and would risk going nuclear.[7] The global antiwar movement, perhaps remembering how the largest protests in history were ignored before the 2003 US-led

---

4   See Jason Bordoff and Meghan L. O'Sullivan, "Green Upheaval: The Geopolitics of Energy," *Foreign Affairs*, January/February 2022; online: https://www.foreignaffairs.com/articles/world/2021-11-30/geopolitics-energy-green-upheaval ; and Henry Sanderson, *Volt Rush: The Winners and Losers in the Race to Go Green* (London: Oneworld Books, 2022).

5   See Jocelyn C. Zuckerman, "For Your Phone and EV, a Cobalt Supply Chain to a Hell on Earth," *Yale Environment 360*, March 30, 2023; online: https://e360.yale.edu/features/siddharth-kara-cobalt-mining-labor-congo; and Fred Pearce, "Why the Rush to Mine Lithium Could Dry Up the High Andes," *Yale Environment 360*, September 19, 2022; online: https://e360.yale.edu/features/lithium-mining-water-andes-argentina.

6   See Idrees Ali and Ted Hesson, "US Four-Star General Warns of War with China in 2025," *Reuters*, 28 January 2023; online: https://www.reuters.com/world/us-four-star-general-warns-war-with-china-2025-2023-01-28/ .

7   A symptomatic social fact: *2034*, the much-discussed *New York Times* best-selling "geopolitical thriller" by Elliot Ackerman and US Admiral (and former NATO commander) James Stavridis, vividly imagines a war between the US and China that escalates to the nuclear bombing of cities. Ackerman and Stavridis, *2034* (New York: Penguin, 2022).

invasion of Iraq, is so far conspicuously missing.

However, diversely motivated revolts and protests have been flaring steadily as the new conjuncture has emerged, many of them undeterred by the Covid-19 pandemic: in Hong Kong (2019-2020), the US (2019-2021), Chile (2019-2022), Bolivia (2019), India (2020-2021), Colombia (2021), Iran (2021-2022), Ecuador (2022), Israel (2023) and France (2018-2020 and 2023), to indicate some of those most reported.[8] Over the last decade, after shelves of dire IPCC reports, high-level foot-dragging at perennial climate summits, and handwringing at Davos, planetary heating has finally entered global public debates – but, as noted, in the form of an official disavowal that leaves the drivers unchanged. Carbon dioxide emissions by the global energy sector grew to a new high in 2022, and Big Oil profits have been soaring.[9] For good measure, another trillion dollars was just invested to open new oil and gas fields over the next seven years.[10]

At the same time, however, and increasingly in the last half-decade, with the arrival of unprecedented extreme weather, heatwaves, droughts, wildfires and floods, news of the planetary has also entered *direct experience*, in both global South and

---

8   See Mikkel Bolt Rasmussen, "Protests After Hegemony," elsewhere in this volume.

9   International Energy Agency (IEA), C02 Emissions in 2022 (March 2023); online: https://www.iea.org/reports/co2-emissions-in-2022; and Jasper Jolly and Jessica Elgot, "Profits at World's Seven Biggest Oil Firms Soar to almost 150bn [British Pounds] this Year," The Guardian, (October 27, 2022); online: https://www.theguardian.com/business/2022/oct/27/profits-at-worlds-seven-biggest-oil-firms-soar-to-almost-150bn-this-year-windfall-tax.

10   "World's Biggest Fossil Fuel Firms Projected to Spend almost a Trillion Dollars on New Oil and Gas Fields by 2030," Global Witness Press Release, April 12, 2022: online: https://www.globalwitness.org/en/press-releases/worlds-biggest-fossil-fuel-firms-projected-to-spend-almost-a-trillion-dollars-on-new-oil-and-gas-fields-by-2030/.

North.[11] This experience is uneven: unequal exposure to impacts and risks reflects the inequalities of global imperialism and its legacies of colonial, gender and racial violence. But this materialism of bodily experience will help to shape a new planetary politics from below – a politics that has the potential to recompose class struggle and reorder the social forcefield.

The "climate crisis" and struggles for climate justice have largely radicalized ecological movements and ecologically-conscious social struggles worldwide. From Standing Rock, La Via Campesina and Black Lives Matter to Ende Gelände, Extinction Rebellion, proliferating ZADs ("Zones to Defend") and Les Soulèvements de la Terre (the uprisings of the earth), the causal root of capitalism and its growth and profit imperatives have been named and challenged, connecting the defense of the biosphere with the intersectional concerns of social justice. Meanwhile, spurred by the urgent need to stop growing greenhouse gas emissions through ever more investment in fixed fossil capital, calls are multiplying for resistance and direct actions against new infrastructure projects; exemplary here is Andreas Malm's much-discussed critique of pacifism, *How to Blow Up a Pipeline*, which will be further disseminated through a new movie of the same name.[12]

Coming in the aftermath of the Left's twentieth-century defeats and misfires, the new conjuncture has been characterized

---

11   By "planetary," I mean the converging crises of climate chaos, species extinction, ecological toxification and zoonotic pandemics, as well as the social crises these produce and the radical political implications that follow. On the general implications for modernist thought and theory, see Dipesh Chakrabarty's elaborated distinction between "global" and "planetary" in *The Climate of History in a Planetary* Age (Chicago: University of Chicago Press, 2021).

12   Andreas Malm, *How To Blow Up a Pipeline: Learning To Fight in a World on Fire* (London: Verso, 2021). The film of the same name, directed by Daniel Goldhaber after a screenplay by Goldhaber, Ariela Barer and Jordan Sjol, was released in cinemas in 2023.

by outrage, revolts and spreading apocalyptic feeling structures but not, so far, by revolutionary movements. Battered by 40 years of neoliberal class war, the revolutionary project of abolishing capitalism has weakened to a hope, anxious and furious by turns, of merely surviving capitalism. But from now on, capitalist realism is precisely the formula for extinction. It is no accident that reconsiderations of vanguard parties and legacies and calls for strategic reflection seem to be ticking up these days; exemplary on the Anglo- and Francophone Left are the long-form journals such as *New Left Review* and, at a quicker tempo in response to unfolding struggles, online media such as *Sidecar*, *Ill Will* and *lundimatin*.

Critiques of the revolutionary vanguard of leftist tradition have typically focused on the vanguard parties, which are deemed to have been too centralized and top-down, insufficiently horizontal and democratic, and productive of subjectivities characterized by a stunted pseudo-autonomy.[13] Typically, the central committee at the top coordinates divisions of political labor, produces strategy and tactics, and issues directives to be executed by disciplined militants. If the modernist State claims a monopoly on legitimate violence, the vanguard claimed a monopoly on the strategic leadership of anti-systemic struggle. Clearly, this model is in disrepute and has largely been abandoned. But this kind of critique of vanguardism risks throwing away the strategic capacity along with the distrusted central committee and party-form.

The stakes here are high: with planetary meltdown compounding nuclearized imperialist rivalry, system change has

---

13   These points, and especially the last, would be the common ground shared by well-known Frankfurt Institute and Situationist critiques of the vanguard parties and their militants, which can be read across the works of Adorno and Debord – and since then has been repeated ad nauseum or merely absorbed as bias.

become doubly existential. Planetary politics from below begins with the rejection of the global: a refusal to be interpellated into capitalist modernization and its nation-states, but also, crucially, a refusal of the calls of anthropocentrism.[14] Before these refusals are processed and articulated rationally, they emerge as feeling structures and passions.[15] The shattering of communities and industrialized exploitation of living beings by state and capital is not limited to humans: diverse more-than-human worlds are also being disappeared. This loss is first registered bodily. Even before it is "worked-through," the distress and anguish over this ecocide works itself into commoner subjectivity as a decisive passional break with modernist extractivism of a desacralized and subordinated "nature."

The *rational* core of planetary politics is in the concept of social metabolism: the capitalist food, energy and water systems; the land uses and transformations; the flows of materials, commodities and people; the urban-weighted techno-material cultures, infrastructures and military-industrial complexes that interact with planetary biophysical systems and drive changes in climate and biodiversity. All this energetics is organized

---

14   I am following here Chakrabarty's distinction between the "global," which implies capitalist modernization but also modernist projects of social progress and which is "humanocentric," and the "planetary," which comes into view with scientific description of climate change and its social drivers and which decenters the human. Chakrabarty, *Climate of History*, pp. 1-92. But whereas Chakrabarty argues that global and planetary scales must from now on be endured together as a "paradox," I conclude that the planetary only becomes political as a refusal of the global (capitalism and its world).

15   It will be recognized that in loosely borrowing Raymond William's concept of "structure of feeling," I am emphasizing what emerges from the complex mix of emotions and passions provoked by direct experience or witnessing of planetary impacts such as extreme weather, toxified ecologies or ravaged landscapes, in combination with encounters, however mediated, of the scientific explanation and political debates. Latent here is a radicalized planetary commoner-subjectivity.

modernity. The metabolic motor is capital accumulation: the economic growth and profit imperatives.

New questions, at once political, ethical and aesthetic, emerge with the new conjuncture described above. These questions, which are easily understood and can be answered without difficulty, go to the crux of livability in the present and the very existence of a future. Does capitalist metabolism undermine the biosphere and promote extinction? Is this metabolism inherently expanding and accelerating? Can capitalism respond to planetary crises by adequately changing and limiting itself, without a revolutionary rupture? The answers (yes, yes, and no), summing up what needs to be known, firmly ground a planetary politics. What the conjuncture calls for is clear, which is not to say easily accomplished. The planetary imperative is: to disarm, power down and abolish capitalism.

Consent for capitalist modernization took the form of "aspiration": access, through consumption, to the glowing world of commodities. Once it is grasped that this modernization has reached its limits and cannot be extended to everyone, let alone sustained – once it is grasped that the smartphone and its world are emphatically unsustainable, insecure and leading to world war and mass extinction – then the understandable hope that everything can remain the same will have to be seen as untenable. Because capitalism's war on the biosphere can no longer be concealed or obfuscated, the failure of its promises of prosperity and security for all is also fully exposed. The actual political divisions today are still confused and do not yet align with the metabolic truths. The Left's job is to see that they do.

Instead of prosperity and security, capitalism is progressively delivering hell on earth. (The images of this hell circulate daily, but as Debord had described, the spectacle – now streaming – saps them of their meaning and import.) The new conjuncture is not one commoners have chosen; it is the one imposed on everyone by capitalist disavowal and intransigence. Planetary politics from below is the rupture that follows, step by step, the argument from social metabolism and all the feelings and passions that accompany it.

The good news is that there are abundant post-growth alternatives to the vicious circle: already existing practices of commoning, agroecology and permaculture, social solidarity, and more-than-human mutuality and symbiosis offer pathways to social metabolisms that are actually sustainable, reparative and resilient. A mutualist and decommodified prosperity is possible: a world repatterned into a plural mosaic of Indigenous communes, instituent autonomist zones, regions and cities of refuge and plurinational eco-socialist federations unbeholden to growth and profits. The bad news, of course, is that capitalism is blocking this "world in which many worlds fit" (or commons of commons) and is prepared to use maximum violence to kill it. It will not be won without a sustained and determined struggle.

Strategies will be needed. Whether or not recoveries or reinventions of vanguard party-forms will also be needed remains to be seen. Leaving that question open, it nevertheless seems clear that the abandonment of the vanguard party-form leaves a strategic void that "diversity of tactics" does not fill. Skepticism is justified, but anti-party dogma is not. In articulating social metabolism, planetary politics and visions of justice into coherent strategies, the vital question would seem to be: how can strategic struggles for a post-capitalist pluriverse be conducted and won without general annihilation? Or does anyone really imagine that capitalism will "die a natural death" that does not entail general annihilation?

Others are reaching similar conclusions. Writing in *Effimera* about the current uprisings in France over pension reductions and the agricultural mega-reservoirs, in a very lucid text translated and reposted on *Ill Will* Maurizio Lazzarato argues that the challenges of recomposing diverse movements and revolts into coordinated strategic struggles can no longer be avoided:

> The lesson to be drawn from these two months of struggle concerns the urgency of rethinking and reconfiguring the question of force, its organization, and its utilization. Tactics and strategy are again becoming political necessities, questions with which movements thus far have tended to overlook, having instead focused almost exclusively on their specific relation to power (sexism, racism, ecology, wages, etc.). Yet, by objectively moving together in the absence of any subjective coordination, they have raised the overall level of confrontation while deconstructing constituted power. Either the problem of the rupture with capitalism and everything it entails will be resolved, or else our actions will remain exclusively defensive.[16]

Reviewing the global cycle of struggles since 2011 and noting the signs of an approaching imperialist world war, Lazzarato also concludes that a new internationalization of strategic struggle may be a necessary response to polycrisis and preventative counter-revolution:

Faced with this tragic and recurrent repetition of wars between imperial powers (not to mention the others), the question we should be asking concerns the reconstruction of international relations of force and the elaboration of a concept of war (which is to say, of strategy) adapted to this new situation.[17]

---

16   Maurizio Lazzarato, "The Class Struggle in France," *Ill Will*, April 15, 2023; online: https://illwill.com/the-class-struggle-in-france.

17   Ibid.

Strategy is historically a terrain of notorious uncertainty, miscalculation and unintended consequences. Working out a planetary strategy for a pathway out of capitalism will need a collective intelligence and social forms to support it (whatever those forms may be). At this point in the argument, I propose three orienting concepts which strategic reflection on the Left should take into account: *metabolic realism*, more-than-human mutuality, and commoning. At the end of the essay, I indicate how they might interact with a Left planetary politics and strategy.

Metabolic Realism

What I am calling *metabolic realism* follows from the discussion of metabolism above and is conceived as a distinguishing antidote to capitalist realism. Metabolic realists have understood that the ever-growing and accelerating social metabolism of capitalist modernity is a threat to the biosphere and its living beings, human and more-than-human. They understand that what is needed is not some diversionary green growth energy transition but rather a *reduction and deceleration of capitalist energetics*, as rapidly as possible, and a reorganization of societal metabolism. And they understand that powering down is not optional: planetary metabolic realities cannot be evaded or escaped.

The hegemony of capitalist realism is breaking up, but it still indicates roughly how much people feel they have to lose or what is in reach for them, within the social status quo. The influence of its perspectives and dispositions weakens as they radiate down from the oligarchic classes and their talking heads. The strategic form of capitalist realism is *geopolitical realism*, which informs the deep traditions and reflexes of the dominant national security paradigm shared by all nation-states and most capitalist class fractions. The assumptions of geopolitical realism were put by Thucydides in the mouths of the Athenians in the infamous Melian Dialogue: in a community of equals, justice might be possible, but in the actual world of inequality, the strong do what they have the power to do, and the weak accept what they must.[18]

In the nation-state system of globalized capitalist economies, such realism compels the maximization of national power, influence and security, as well as profits. As noted, the results today are a new climate imperialism tending toward climate fascism and a third world war. For both state and capital, the risks that would come with another world war would seem to be preferable to any real change in social power relations or in the economic logic of capitalism. Unfortunately for them, war will not solve their metabolic crisis.

Their absolute investment in the status quo leads the ruling classes to disavow metabolic realities and to hope for rescue by magical technologies – a disposition that can only be called *metabolic delusion*. This delusion is a wager, not a strategy. If nuclear fusion and other hyped technologies fail to roll out or to work as planned, then that wager will have been an existential blunder. What could justify an intransigence based, when all is said and done, on hopes of outflanking the laws of thermodynamics? Planetary heating and climate chaos began as unintended consequences. But what can it mean, to persist down that path decades after the drivers and impacts have been understood? To answer that the growth imperative is "locked-in" by the requirements of our technologies only begs the question: what good is the smartphone and its world, if they are baking the biosphere and unraveling the webs of life?

---

18   The corollary is: the strong rule as much as they can, for as long as they can. See Thucydides, *History of the Peloponnesian War*, trans. Rex Warner (New York: Penguin Books, 1972), 400-408.

The politics of planetary commoners, by contrast, does not presume a pact with delusion. Planetary commoners only need to bring social justice goals into alignment with metabolic realism. Grounding Left strategy in metabolic realism means a commitment to reducing the energetics and reserving growth for selected collective needs.[19] It means re-evaluating modernization and its state- and capital-controlled regimes of technology development. More, it means refusing the whole geopolitical framework of capitalist nation-states. This will be crucial as war spreads and all are called to join the war effort under their side's flag. Between metabolic realism and capitalist realism there is only a revolutionary rupture. "No planetary justice, no peace" would be its expression.

More-Than-Human Mutuality

All the living-beings of the Holocene biosphere – an evolutionary community to which the human species is a relative newcomer – are threatened by capitalist modernity's anti-planetary metabolism. "An injury to one is an injury to all" is not just a slogan of social solidarity; today it also expresses ecological connectivity and relationality. The modernist construction of a subordinating separation between humans and "nature" set up a project of mastery in which state, capital, science and technology were all mobilized in a 500-year history of ecocidal extractions and dumpings, as well as genocidal destructions of communities deemed less than or incompletely

---

19   On degrowth, see inter alia: Mark Burton and Peter Somerville, "Degrowth: A Defense," *New Left Review*, no. 115, 2019, 95-104; Jason Hickel, "Degrowth: A Theory of Radical Abundance," *Real-World Economics Review*, no. 87, 2019, 54-68; Matthias Schmelzer, Aaron Vansintjan and Andrea Vetter, *The Future Is Degrowth: A Guide to a World Beyond Capitalism* (London: Verso, 2022); and Kate Soper, *Post-Growth Living: For an Alternative Hedonism* (London: verso, 2020).

"human." Terminating these development narratives entails delegitimating anthropocentrism.

This conceptual relation to what used to be called nature (but what can now be parsed as the biosphere and planet) provided ideological cover for a metabolism that expanded and accelerated like an "automatic subject."[20] But anthropocentrism does not hold up either empirically or theoretically. Humans are part of the biosphere, but emphatically are not in control of it. Species boundaries are a heuristic device rather than policeable borders: the bodies of each one of us are compositions of multi-species symbiosis.[21]

It will not be enough, to oppose capitalist economic relations while leaving the anthropocentric modernist relation to biosphere and planet unchanged. A repatterning of metabolism needs to be supported by repatterned feeling structures. A sense of respect, kinship and mutuality with more-than-human living beings – whether recovered from local traditions, learned from Indigenous comrades or appropriated from evolutionary science – begins as a feeling structure but reflects a decisive passional break with the modernist body of extractivism and exterminism.[22]

---

20   The phrase is from Marx's discussion of the General Formula for *Capital from Capital: A Critique of Political Economy*, vol. 1, trans. Ben Fowkes (New York: Vintage Books, 1977), 255.

21   See Scott F. Gilbert, Jan Sapp and Alfred I. Tauber, "A Symbiotic View of Life: We Have Never Been Individuals," *Quarterly Review of Biology*, vol. 87, no. 4, 2012, 325-341; and, more generally, Donna J. Haraway, *Staying with the Trouble: Making Kin in the Chthulucene* (Durham: Duke University Press, 2016.

22   I follow the intentionally humbling formulation of David Abrams, who speaks of nature more simply and reverently as the "more-than-human." See Abrams, *Becoming Animal: An Earthly Cosmology* (New York: Vintage, 2011) and *The Spell of the Sensuous: Perception and Language in a More-Than-Human World* (New York: Vintage, 1997).

Re-enchantment, as Silvia Federici notes, can be a form of political resistance to a modernist disenchantment that reduces all beings and things to fungible commodities or unwanted superfluities.[23] There is no need to prescribe or try to predict the diverse forms in which re-enchanted feeling structures will appear and be lived: either the practices and ceremonies are already there, as at Standing Rock, or else they will be found or invented as locally needed, as they were on the ZAD in Notre-Dame-des-Landes.[24]

Of course, a fully realized planetary reconciliation between all living beings is an impossible ideal: some antagonisms between species will necessarily persist, even in what Anna Tsing names the "latent commons."[25] But a commitment to as much mutual flourishing and more-than-human symbiosis as possible is already a needed paradigm change. The proposition here is that such a feeling structure and commitment will be part of leftwing planetary commoner-subjectivity. When embodied as material force, these can become a strategic strength.[26]

---

23   See Silvia Federici, *Re-enchanting the World: Feminism and the Politics of the Commons* (Oakland: PM Press, 2019), 188-189.

24   On art and ceremonies on the ZAD, see Isabelle Fremeaux and Jay Jordan, *We Are 'Nature' Defending Itself* (London: Pluto, 2021).

25   See Anna Lowenhaupt Tsing, *The Mushroom at the End of the World: On the Possibility of Life in Capitalist Ruins* (Princeton: Princeton University Press, 2015), 134-135 and 255.

26   Marx famously wrote that radical theory becomes a material force when it grips the masses. My point is that feeling structures are not separate from theory, behind some cordon sanitaire; they interact with and embody it.

Commoning

Commons are local, mutualist associations of direct producers.[27] In Massimo De Angelis' account, "commons systems" are composed of three elements: commoners, common goods (or "use-values for a plurality"), and the practices of commoning by which these goods are produced.[28] Beyond this, the commons has no single, fixed form; it is reinvented each time by the commoners who come together to provision and produce common goods. Commons systems can be linked up into larger-scale "commons ecologies," through the transformation that De Angelis calls "commonization."[29]

Commoning is an appropriate form for beginning to repattern the social metabolism with the planet on a local level – and to do so with metabolic realism, against the unplanetary imperatives of capitalist realism. Commoning opens zones of mutualist, de-commodified relations and does not require continuous growth and acceleration. Forms of more-than-human commoning are especially urgent to learn and explore. Local food systems established as commons and based on practices of agroecology, permaculture or other forms of reparative, resilient and sustainable provisioning are excellent and available examples of applied metabolic realism.

---

27   The object of intense theoretical reflection over the last several decades, the concept of the commons and the political principle of the common have mapped out a zone of social struggle and construction that is neither public nor private, neither state nor capitalist economy. I discuss the commons and its growing literature, including more-than-human commoning, in *After the Holocene: Planetary Politics for Commoners* (forthcoming), op. cit.

28   Massimo De Angelis, *Omnia Sunt Communia: On the Commons and the Transformation to Postcapitalism* (London: Zed Books, 2017), 29.

29   Ibid., 10-15, 77-117, 273-274.

Moreover, commoning makes strategic sense: as a form of mutualist preparation for capitalist modernity's metabolic failures, commoning is prudent and practical insurance that aligns well with strategic abolitionist aims. It would also be exemplary of strategic indirection: a "commons of commons," or commons ecologies, could be built in relative safety, below the radar or even off the grid, in most cases without immediate confrontation with the repressive agencies of systemic enforcement. Commoning is therefore strategically appropriate for a Left in need of time and space for recomposing, reskilling, rethinking and strategizing. I return to this below.

Knowing the Enemy

Above, I bluntly formulated the planetary imperative: to disarm, power down and abolish capitalism. Considering these allegedly unimaginable tasks, I'm well aware that merely to state these aims as necessity will appear outlandishly unrealistic. Who could possibly realize them, and how? Isn't this just rhetoric? To *disarm* capitalism would mean to disarm the dominant nation-states. Given that this is hardly a new goal and that the Left is perhaps as weak as it has ever been exactly as the state is militarily stronger than ever, isn't this absurd overreach? To *power down* capitalism would be to confront and constrain its core laws of motion: the imperatives of growth and accumulation. How likely is this, when the actually emerging Green energy transition aims to sustain profitable growth by powering up to grow better? And *abolish*? That would mean the decisive displacement of capitalism's global dominance and a deep social, economic, political and cultural repatterning. Is such ambition not laughable?

It would be, perhaps, in the absence of compounding planetary crises and what I elsewhere referred to as "the non-linear fury of the planet itself."[30] But pointing to this wild card is not a strategy, not an adequate or just planetary politics, not a plausible pathway out of capitalist modernity to a better world. It merely marks the fact that capital and state are not all-powerful, that there is no magical escape from the Real of earthly metabolism, and that the ruling classes are quite capable of fatal strategic mistakes: after the Holocene, the stakes, challenges and risks are existential all around.

The 2022 Biden-Harris US National Security Strategy openly admits as much.[31] It also acknowledges that a new round of inter-imperialist rivalry has begun. It is worth reviewing some key points of this document, as it reveals much about the brittle rigidities and looming fears of the climate imperialist mind. The "post-Cold War period [read: in which US state and capital called the shots from a position of unipolar hegemony] is definitively over and a competition is underway between the major powers to shape what comes next."[32] The "inflection point" of the coming decade will be decisive: "The window of opportunity to deal with shared threats, like

---

30   See Ray, *After the Holocene: Planetary Politics for Commoners* (forthcoming), op. cit.

31   *National Security Strategy* (Washington, D.C.: The White House, 2022), 9: "Of all the shared problems we face, climate change is the greatest and potentially existential for all nations." Or again, with zero equivocation, 27: "The climate crisis is the existential crisis of our time."

32   Ibid., p. 6. In this periodization, "post-Cold War" corresponds roughly to the period of accelerating neoliberal globalization under US hegemony. No attempt is made to clarify exactly why this international "order" reached its limit, but the answers would have obvious pertinency. Wherever the "geopolitical" is invoked in this document or in the national security discourse of the last several years, we can read: intensified imperialist rivalry.

climate change, will narrow drastically." Two rivals, no surprise, are singled out: China and Russia.[33]

The new trope for selling climate imperialism turns out to be much like the old trope: the so-called democracies stand against the autocrats. (In the politics of spectacle, as in the unconscious, contradiction and inconsistencies are no problem.) US military preeminence, unmatched in history, will be maintained, the strategists declare, "with the PRC as its pacing challenge."[34] Technology is counted as a vital interest and decisive geopolitical factor, and continuing US dominance in this sector will be supported and secured.[35]

The energy transition away from fossil fuels gets five paragraphs under the heading "Climate and Energy Security." The details are vague and subject to politics, but it will happen in some form, eventually. Meanwhile, the US will act with allies and partners "to ensure energy security and affordability, secure access to critical mineral supply chains, and ensure a just

---

33   Ibid., 8: The People's Republic of China is "the only competitor with both the intent to reshape the international order and, increasingly, the economic, diplomatic, military and technological power to advance that objective."

34   Ibid., p. 20. As has been the case for many years, annual US military spending ($816.7 billion allotted for 2023) exceeds that of all its closest rivals and allies combined. See online: https://www.defense.gov/News/News-Stories/Article/Article/3252968/biden-signs-national-defense-authorization-act-into-law/. This will likely be changing, though, as a result of Putin's invasion of Ukraine. The member states of NATO, and notably France and Germany, have announced major increases in military spending, as has China.

35   Ibid., 32-33: "In the next decade, critical and emerging technologies are poised to retool economies, transform militaries, and reshape the world."

transition for impacted workers."[36] This, then, is the Green New Deal after editing by Homeland Security and Joe Manchin and passed by Congress as the Inflation Reduction Act of 2022. Fossil fuels will be around for decades to come, with all that this implies for global heating and species extinction. Such are the burdens of defending the capitalist classes.

With regard to terrorism, the threats are now deemed "more ideologically diverse and geographically diffuse than that of two decades ago. Al-Qa'ida, ISIS, and associated forces have expanded from Afghanistan and the Middle East into Africa and Southeast Asia."[37] No end for the forever war on terror, then – though this will be conducted more covertly, through drone strikes and special ops with allies rather than large-scale shock and awe. Biden's 2021 withdrawal from Afghanistan, confirming in the world's eyes that land's historic reputation as a "graveyard of empire," is boldly claimed as the "victory" of justice delivered to Bin Laden.[38] "Meanwhile," the document continues, "we face sharply increased threats from a range of domestic violent extremists here in the United States."[39]

All in all, these are worrying times for the global hegemon. Swagger and bluster are gone, but in the wake the house is divided against itself. The storied "American way of life" was once held up as the very paradigm of modernist aspirations: these days the open road, in all its bulleted, awakened and detonating self-conflicts, devolves into horror show. Over the horizon a rival is

---

36   Ibid., 28.

37   Ibid., 30.

38   Ibid.

39   Ibid. The reference of course is to rightwing and white supremacist militias, fight clubs and terror groups such as the Base, Atomwaffen Division, the Proud Boys and the Oathkeepers, members of which were also actively involved in the storming of the US Capitol on 6 January 2021.

rising, emboldening others. Threats foreseen and unpredicted are complexifying everywhere. Allies and partners will be more needed but are making their own calculations.

What is asserted is a somewhat humbled yet grim determination to hold on to the leading position, to defend perceived vital interests at all costs, and to use all assets and advantages to dominate rivals in the unfolding "polycrisis." We might remember what Thucydides has the Athenians say at Sparta before the declaration of war: "We acted just as everyone does, when we accepted the empire that was offered to us. And now that you distrust and fear us, it has become too dangerous for us to let it go."[40] But if the melancholy of late imperialist realism pervades the performances of the Biden Administration, this is hardly evidence that US decline is imminent. The power to inflict damage, punishment and death is visibly and indisputably intact. And neither the capitalist class nor great powers will go gently into that dark night.

The 2022 National Security Plan is a reminder, however, that moods, fears, anxieties, melancholy, the memory of losses and scars of defeats imprinted on bodies and minds, and other sinew-sapping blows to confidence all enter too into the balance of forces – as the Left should know better than anyone.[41] (In the old strategic treatises, the stability of feeling-structures was discussed under the notion of "morale.")

---

40   Thucydides, *History of the Peloponnesian War*, op. cit., 79-80, my paraphrase.

41   The mood in Washington is not shared in Beijing, however. Xi Jinping's "China Dream" is a rising power's projection of confidence. Unlike Trump's MAGA, Xi's vision to "Make China Great Again" flows from an awakened sense of national destiny. See Graham Allison, *Destined for War: Can America and China Escape the Thucydides Trap* (Melbourne: Scribe Publications, 2017).

Commoning and Planetary Politics

Finding each other and making common cause, sharing experiences, deepening bonds and spreading skills, planetary commoners have a chance to learn what can be done in worsening conditions – and done better than competitive capitalist markets. When by quiet trial and error commoners have learned and shown this to themselves, when they have grown confident in their power to provision, produce and repattern well and convivially at local scale, then others will take notice. And well-made and cared-for commons systems will tend to connect and grow into commons ecologies, as De Angelis describes.[42]

Simply by making and sharing and taking care, commoners prepare for modernity's metabolic meltdowns. By their mutualist preparations, they build networks of practical refuge and sanctuary. If these by miracle are not needed in some places, then nothing lost: the "use-values for a plurality" that commoning produces are their own reward.[43] If refuges are needed, as any kind of realism must expect, then by this path of mutual production and support, commoners enter the balance and in time become factors in the forcefield. This vision of more-than-human mutuality and reparative "mitigation" from below would be degrowth in action.[44]

Commoning in itself would of course not suffice to displace or abolish capital. These are first steps, not endgame. But these first steps toward resilience and autonomy are makeable moves, here and now, in a planetary politics: they are steps on a path by which oppositional culture can be recovered and

---

42   De Angelis, *Omnia Sunt Communia*, op. cit., 287-289.

43   The quoted phrase is from Ibid., 29.

44   For discussion of more-than-human commoning, see Ray, *After the Holocene: Planetary Politics for Commoners* (forthcoming), op. cit.

sheltered and struggles recomposed in relative safety and with minimal risk. They will lead to next steps and to steps up in scale. A plural mosaic of common forms, on the way to a metabolically realistic "world of many worlds."

What stands in the way of such a vision? What prevents such steps and the making of commoners? This essay has sketched some realistic assessments: of capitalist modernity's failing energetics and metabolism, of the hardships these failures will continue to bring, and of the depths of transformation needed to slow, cope and survive the loss of the Holocene. Nor has a realistic overview of the larger conjunctural obstacles been evaded: the headlock and military supremacy of imperialist modernity, and the present strategic weakness of the Left. But hardship, the intransigence of the climate imperialist classes, and the dearth of compelling strategies from the Left are fertile ground for the commons. Planetary pressures not only favor the spread of commoning, they all but compel it. As argued above, commoning as precaution and insurance makes perfect sense and is fully compatible with abolitionist aims.[45]

What prevents the emergence of commoners, then? Fear of failure, the contempt of consumers, the sarcasm of big-tractor communists? How about fear that successes will be co-opted, or will attract attacks by supremacist militias or state repression as punitive example? In some places and situations, these last two possibilities could be a serious deterrent. But lack of land is undoubtedly the greatest impediment to getting started. Capitalist property relations and real estate markets – the whole legalized, normalized aftermath of land grabs and

---

45   I use "abolition" in this essay to refer not only to the prison and police abolition movement now associated with Black Lives Matter protests and racial justice discourse, but more generally to the traditional Left aim of abolishing "the present state of things," in the sense of a radical repatterning of the whole social process (capitalist modernity), rather than some of its parts.

enclosures – are by definition hostile to the mutualism of commoners, even if commoning movements are not yet "locked-on" by the targeting systems of security agencies.[46] Back to land and Land Back, then: access to land, in support of and alliance with Indigenous struggles for reparation, should return to the core of Left politics. And it will do, as modernist metabolism unravels. For the landless, the way ahead will be harder and riskier, but the ZAD in France and MST (Movement of Landless Workers) in Brazil offer inspiring examples of what can be done, North and South.

For those who do have access to land, the wager of commoning is a good one – as first steps toward re-grounding, food and energy sovereignty, and material mutual support. Eventually of course, commons and commoners will be drawn into political conflicts. Even the humblest part-time local commons must come into being in a context of social antagonism and in close proximity to the threat of conflict and clashing. There is no denying this, or the marked drift toward increasing violence, at both national and international scales. Even pursuing careful paths of strategic indirection, the problem of self-defense will sooner or later be forced on commoners.[47]

---

46   At least in the North, where permaculture, crafting and Transition Towns are mostly seen as harmless hobbies. I discuss Land Back in relation to agroecology and permaculture in *After the Holocene: Planetary Politics for Commoners* (forthcoming), op. cit.

47   On the problems and dilemmas of self-defense, see the lucid new work by Elsa Dorlin, *Self-Defense: A Philosophy of Violence* (London: Verso, 2022), and in particular her critical genealogy of Krav Maga.

On Violence

It is not plausible to expect that capital will be disarmed either by electoral politics or by main force. It seems far more likely that the state's powers of violence and terror will be neutralized when soldiers and officers refuse to fight – presumably, when a deepened crisis of legitimacy becomes acute. A dual power scenario, for example, when metabolic failures and imperial defeats are matched by the rising power of a coordinated plurality of commons-forms.[48] That scenario won't arrive automatically. Nor will it arrive gently and peacefully.

There has never been and will never be a capitalism without violence. Its constructive innovations have gone hand in hand with its destructive frenzies, its marvels of science bound to its powers of terror. Modernity's awesome energetics was in the end a climate and evolution bomb. "All that" is reaching its metabolic terminus in the emergence of the planetary. In that ending and emergence, violence will not be avoidable. The intransigence of capital and the national security state guarantee this. But if violence is unavoidable, it can still be limited and contained by strategies of indirection and the refusal of the worst.

To reflect again on the problem of violence – of the state, war and terror – I return to two texts that have long spurred my thinking: Retort's *Afflicted Powers* and T.J. Clark's "For a Left

---

48   In *After the Holocene: Planetary Politics for Commoners* (forthcoming), op. cit., I draw on De Angelis and Nicos Poulantzas to sketch a forcefield of *quadrupal power*, to take into account the possible growth of commons ecologies. In it, four distinct forms of organized power are in play: (1) *capital*, the driver of modernist metabolism, presently dominates the field. Its economic imperatives and processes are backstopped and generally supported by (2) *the state*. Oppositional demands and pressure from below are generated by (3) *working class and social movements*. Quietly organizing an alternative metabolism from below are (4) *commons ecologies*, or networked associations of local commons systems.

with No Future."[49] In their long, intersecting engagements with the history and present of leftwing politics, Retort and Clark have registered trenchant critiques of modernity, vanguardism, capitalist spectacle and the permanent warfare state. *Afflicted Powers*, penned by Iain Boal, T.J. Clark, Joseph Matthews and Michael Watts, brilliantly reads the deep motors and contexts of the terror atrocities of September 11, 2001, and the US-led so-called war on terror that followed. "For a Left with No Future" draws hard conclusions from the Left's failures to respond effectively to the 2007/8 global financial meltdown and bailouts. Both texts deserve to be re-read and studied in the light of the planetary condition, as the losses of the Holocene climate and biodiversity take hold. The outlines of a leftist critique of modernity sketched in both texts remain pertinent.

In analyzing al-Qaida as a product of the deep structures and longer waves of modernist imperialism, Retort insists on the dense imbrication of capital, spectacle and war across the twentieth and into the twenty-first century. And war, one sharp end of that unholy triad, is in turn in bound to the state and to modernity.[50] To paraphrase the argument, the war-machine is motored by, and in turn enforces, a specific social nexus or complex: capital-spectacle-state-modernity. The "military neo-liberalism" of mercenary transnationals, outsourced ops, and the war zone services sector was one of its new mutations.[51] For both Retort and Clark, the emergence of al-Qaida as a new vanguard of terror channeling the rage of immiserated masses

---

49   T.J. Clark, "For a Left with No Future," *New Left Review*, no. 74, 2012, 53-75; reprinted with modifications in *Heaven on Earth: Painting and the Life to Come* (London: Thames & Hudson, 2018), 237-262; and Retort (Iain Boal, T.J. Clark, Joseph Matthews and Michael Watts), *Afflicted Powers: Capital and Spectacle in a New Age of War* (London: Verso, 2005).

50   Retort, *Afflicted Powers*, 78-79.

51   Ibid., 72.

in the slums of mega-cities, was "the state's ticket to ride."[52] Nothing since then refutes this. Decisively rejecting militant vanguardism of all flags, whether practiced by the modernist parties of the Left or the antimodernist bombers of Islamic extremism, Retort calls for "an opposition to modernity having nothing to do with al-Qaida's."[53] Further qualifications of this notion are offered: "A non-orthodox, non-nostalgic, non-rejectionist, non-apocalyptic critique of the modern: that ought now to be the task of Left politics. Otherwise the ground of opposition to the present will be permanently ceded to one or another fundamentalism."[54] There would be much to discuss regarding the critique of modernity called for. But the argument of *Afflicted Powers* confirms at minimum that neither terror nor direct attacks on symbolic fortresses of the capital-spectacle-war-state-modernity complex can be winning strategies for the Left.

Clark controversially pushes this conclusion further – and, for quite a few critics, too far.[55] Clark calls for the Left to look defeat in the face and deepen its critical reconstruction of the enlightenment project.[56] The whole texture and tonality of Left politics, he argues, now needs to be "transposed into a

---

52   Clark, "For a Left with No Future," 75; *Heaven on Earth*, 262: "Extremism, to repeat, is the state's ticket to ride."

53   Retort, *Afflicted Powers*, 177.

54   Ibid.

55   See Mikkel Bolt Rasmussen, "A Nightmare on the Brains of the Living: Repeating the Past and Imagining a Future," *Nordic Journal of Aesthetics*, no. 49-50, 2015, 91-117; Alberto Toscano, "Politics in a Tragic Key," *Radical Philosophy*, no. 180, 2013, 25-34; and Susan Watkins, "Presentism? A Reply to T.J. Clark," *New Left Review*, no. 74, 2012, 77-102.

56   Clark, "For a Left with No Future," 56; *Heaven on Earth*, 241: "'How far down?' Some of us think, 'Seven levels of the world'."

tragic key" – one adjusted to the disaster of deep defeat and in keeping with a more disabused "sense of the horror and danger built into human affairs."[57] Uttering heresies, Clark wants the Left to be done with its "big ideas" and "revolutionary stylistics" and to leave behind "the whole grain and frame of its self-conception, the last afterthoughts and images of the avant-garde."[58]

Having defined the Left as "root and branch opposition to capitalism," Clark utters the greatest heresy of all:

The question of capitalism – precisely because the system itself is once again posing (agonizing over) the question, and therefore its true enormity emerges from behind the shadow play of parties – has to be bracketed. It cannot be made political. The Left should turn its attention to what can.[59]

Although mindful of this assertion, I must refuse its substance. What does it mean to claim that the question of capitalism cannot be made political? It would be one thing to say: the Left is too weak at present to offer a systemic challenge, enough with the chatter about revolution. But the formula is not qualified it all: the wording is categorical and absolute. Unless the "tragic key" means that the Left should be willing to swallow its root and branch opposition and bitterly abide with capitalism all the way down to biospheric ruin and extinction, we will have to refuse this passage or interpret it to mean something else. Perhaps this: since revolution according to the vanguardist template evidently no longer inspires support, the Left should put what oppositional energies it can muster into different forms of politics – or into inventing better templates for

---

57   Clark, "For a Left with No Future," 57 and 60; *Heaven on Earth*, 242 and 245.

58   Clark, "For a Left with No Future," 57; *Heaven on Earth*, 241 and 242.

59   Clark, "For a Left with No Future," 54 and 55; *Heaven on Earth*, 238 and 239.

revolutionary practice. That is not so easy to do, but if this is what Clark means, then in fairness it must be said that many on the Left have been trying.

Clark's challenge is premised on a sense of human capacities and propensities for extreme violence. Indeed, in the new key: for "evil." And, additionally, on a healthy appreciation for unpredictable consequences, for blow-back, for the damage and vicious circles that mistakes, miscalculations and overreach can cause and let loose. What kind of practical politics did Clark propose instead, in 2012? One that, he argues, "can co-exist fully with the most modest, most moderate, of materialisms."[60] It is wrong, he elaborates:

to assume that moderacy in politics, if we mean by this a politics of small steps, bleak wisdom, concrete proposals, disdain for grand promises, a sense of the hardness of even the least "improvement," is not *revolutionary* – assuming this last word has any descriptive force left. It depends on what the small steps are aimed at changing. It depends on the picture of human possibility in the case. A politics actually directed, step by step, failure by failure, to preventing the tiger from charging out would be the most moderate and revolutionary there has ever been.[61]

At the end of the essay, by way of further elaboration, Clark returns to the concept of "the permanent warfare state" introduced by Retort in *Afflicted Powers*.[62] Now Clark proposes

---

60   Clark, "For a Left with No Future," 63; *Heaven on Earth*, 249.

61   Clark, "For a Left with No Future," 67; *Heaven on Earth*, 253, Clark's italics. The repeated use of the term "politics" in this passage begs the question: the possibility of a moderate but revolutionary (in his sense) politics would refute, would it not, the earlier claim that "the question of capitalism. . . cannot be made political"?

62   Clark, "For a Left with No Future," 74; *Heaven on Earth*, 261.

that the Left's traditional focus on inequality and social injustice would be reenergized by such a reorientation toward the containment of state violence. The reorientation is not, note, toward liberal or moral pacifism: the politics he is envisioning begins by accepting unequivocally that "Peace will never happen."[63] Antagonism, to paraphrase, will never be wholly eliminated by social engineering. (And to recall where we are now in 2023: in planetary meltdown all antagonisms are intensifying.) Clark stresses that "the focal point, the always recurring center of [Left] politics, should be to contain the effects and extent of warfare, and to try (the deepest revolutionary demand) to prise aggressivity and territoriality apart from their nation-state form. Piece by piece; against the tide; interminably."[64]

An interesting proposition: to bracket the political question of capitalism while working patiently and diligently at disarming it. In this conception, to be consistent, the work of disarming no longer counts as political; but of course it cannot but be political, and Clark in fact ends by proposing anti-militarism as, exactly, a "politics." To understand him better, we can reread the final chapter of *Afflicted Powers*, titled "Modernity and Terror." Given the logics of the permanent warfare state complex, linking the state and its war machine to capital, spectacle and deep modernity, Retort argues there, a politics focused on the network of some 750 US military bases operating beyond US borders would "challenge the whole texture of modernity."[65]

Opposition to the world of bases – "a perfectly standard (and urgent) item of anti-militarism and anti-imperialism" – opens onto the whole question of state power in its closest, and most

---

63   Ibid.

64   Ibid.

65   Retort, *Afflicted Powers*, 189.

closely guarded, relations to capitalist modernity.[66] At the capitalist root of that modernity is a process of tireless enclosure and episodic primitive accumulations: these processes are not the exploitative thefts of time in the hourly wage or the invisible arbitrage of algorithmic trading. Enclosure and primitive accumulation are open violence and terror. That is why the nation-state as the agency of enforcement has been so necessary to both capital and modernity as such. "*Bases are the state incarnate*, it soon becomes clear: they embody the state in its extra-territorial sovereignty, its lawmaking and lawbreaking will."[67]

Abu Ghraib and Guantanamo (one of the infamous Abu Ghraib photographs was chosen as the frontispiece to *Afflicted Powers*), the cages, hoods and orange jumpsuits, the waterboarders and apparatus of extraordinary rendition, reveal precisely how the state violence generated by capitalist modernity has mutated since World War II:

Bases are a thousand points of darkness: a lymphatic system pumping out antibodies to the rule of law and the remaining (dim) possibility of democratic control. They are a shadow anticipation of the earth as one vast arena of "covert operations" and the "indefinite exercise of extra-legal state control."[68]

The argument is compelling. To roll back the network of US military bases – and neither China nor Russia has or is seriously trying to construct anything comparable – would indeed

---

66   Ibid.

67   Ibid., 189-190, Retort's italics. Here the argument converges well with Giorgio Agamben's analysis of the camp as a condensation of modernity's violence. See Agamben, "What Is a Camp?" in *Means without End: Notes on Politics*, trans. Vincenzo Binetti and Cesare Casarino (Minneapolis: University of Minnesota Press, 2000), 37-44.

68   Retort, *Afflicted Powers*, 190. The quoted phrases are from Judith Butler, *Precarious Life: The Powers of Mourning and Violence* (London: Verso, 2004), 64.

be a radically transformative disarming of capitalism. And the "absolute" resistance encountered whenever the closure of even one base becomes an object of politics – think of Okinawa, think of Guantanamo, which appallingly remains open to this day – evinces "the enormity of what is challenged when bases are called into question."[69]

And just as Marx's concept of primitive accumulation is only fully grasped when, revised, it is carried forward in time from early colonial modernity and recognized as a still-contemporary process, so the networks of camps and military bases, I suggest, should be projected back into the early-modern violence of the settler colonial frontier.[70] But this implies, to détourn E.P. Thompson, that the Base is not a Thing.[71] It must be understood, rather, as a condensation of social relations and processes, whose germ-form was perhaps the settler colonial "fort" from which genocides of Indigenous inhabitants were launched and land grabs by settlers defended, but which continued to develop through a long series of historically-specific mutations. In other words, as I read Retort, the point of the focus on bases is that opposition directed there brings the whole systemic problem, including its capitalist root, into view: capitalist modernity as a "total

---

69   Retort, *Afflicted Powers*, 190. The paragraph continues: "The challenge in any one case will be local. 'national,' commonsensical, phrased in a variety of idioms. But the resistance to it, on the part of sovereign power, will be absolute; and the absolutism of the resistance will itself be a lesson in what bases are, and to what political and economic – not simply military – necessities they answer."

70   The key text in the revision of "so-called original accumulation" is Midnight Notes Collective, "The New Enclosures," in *Midnight Oil: Work, Energy, War, 1973-1992* (Brooklyn: Autonomedia, 1992).

71   E.P. Thompson, "Notes on Exterminism, the Last Stage of Civilization," in *Exterminism and Cold War, ed. New Left Review* (London: Verso, 1982), 3-5.: "The Bomb is, after all, something more than an inert Thing." This essay resonates anew in light of the post-Holocene extinctions.

social process," or in Retort's terms, the capital-spectacle-war-state-modernity complex.

With the resurgence of the planetary, I have argued here, the main focus must shift to capitalist metabolism and energetics. We on the Left have no choice, unless we spurn survival, but to take the problem of metabolism in our hands. And we can reach the local interfaces of that metabolism and begin to slow and relax them through commoning. As planetary commoners, not green consumers. But we must reach the driver of modernist metabolism, too: we cannot bracket the question of capitalism in an adequate planetary politics.

As Retort and Clark suggest, there are still pressure points in these systems. And political opposition must aim itself against these. Many points, in fact, come into view with each imperative task. *Power down*: "the airport and its world" (to borrow a slogan from the ZAD), the dam, the pipeline, the man-camp, the mine, the container port, the factory farm, the smartphone – and their world. *Disarm*: the base and its world, nuclear weapons and WMDs, the armed drone, state secrecy, surveillance, the arms trade, the prison, the police. *Abolish*: growth and its world, the WTO, Big Tech, the transnational corporation, the commodities market, debt, dark money, the billionaire class (the 1%), the tax haven, the revolving door.

There are more, obviously – too many. To be effective, would it not be better to focus on just one or three of these? But how to choose? As the planet heats, is the base world still that vital point of the total social process? Should disarming capital be given priority? Arguably, yes. Bases condense and reveal a globalized power to wage war; and war, in its toxic energetics no less than its terrible killing, is biospheric disaster. The globalizing disasters of open war, we can already see from the fallout over Putin's brutal invasion of Ukraine, will overwhelm and undo international focus and cooperation on climate response.

In open war, as identities are threatened, enmities hardened and vicious circles of vengeance allowed to turn, the conditions of mutualist co-inhabitation are also put to fire. The urgency of checking the drift toward a third world war could not be clearer. Obviously enough, closing bases, reducing military budgets, abolishing WMDs and containing the arms industries are necessary parts of a planetary politics and strategy – and yet all the dominant nation-states are now racing in the opposite direction.[72]

Can the Left come together around a small number of strategic urgencies, instead of endlessly spilling its remnant energies into the infinite menu of causes? The Left seems to have become allergic to all prioritizing and to have given up on reaching a more coordinated strategy: no struggle, one hears today, can have priority over the others. For some, it seems, even to propose the need for a strategy smacks of the bad old vanguardism. That conclusion I think needs to be revisited: the indifference it invites is strategic doom. To assess, discuss and debate the tasks, the pressure points, the strategies, the tactics – and to do it with metabolic realism and rigor: this would be evidence of a planetary politics serious enough to inspire some confidence.

How, to return to the problems of violence and self-defense, can such a planetary politics be conducted, without confrontations escalating to total war? In a period where politics is again becoming fixed on identities – and above all national, racial and religious ones – the risk is large that political differences

---

72   As I write this, the war in Ukraine is still escalating, the economic competition between the USA and China is still militarizing, and global military spending rose by 3.7% and has reached an historic high of $2.24 trillion. See Ana Assis, Nan Tian, Diego Lopez da Silva, Xiao Liang, Lorenzo Scarazzato and Lucie Béraud-Sudreau, *Trends in World Military Expenditure, 2022* (Stockholm: SIPRI, April 2023).

will be experienced as existential threats. And worse, will do so with no or little mediation, in a short circuit that obliterates the common of shared worlds and planet: you don't look like me, I shoot you first. The supremacist politics of Great Replacements. Most dangerous here are the existential fears of the top capitalists: they well perceive that a planetary politics poses an existential threat to their class power and privilege. We need to avoid giving them any special reasons to fear for their lives as well.[73]

Back to Clark's "For a Left with No Future," for some clarification on what must be expected:

It surely goes without saying that *a movement of opposition* of the kind I have been advocating, the moment it began to register even limited successes, would call down the full crude fury of the state on its head. The boundaries between *political organizing* and armed resistance would break down – not of the Left's choosing, but as a simple matter of self-defense. Imagine if a movement really began to put the question of the permanent war economy back on the table – in however limited a way, with however symbolic a set of victories. Be assured that the brutality of the "kettle" would be generalized. The public order helicopters would be on their way back from Bahrain. Jean Charles de Menezes would have many brothers.[74]

---

73   Expropriation does not entail physical extermination. The more planetary meltdown is recognized as a termination of capitalist modernity, the more the Left needs to make clear its rejection of all forms of exterminism.

74   Clark, "For a Left with No Future," 74; *Heaven on Earth*, 261-262, my italics. I've picked out these phrases to emphasize that Clark ends with a politics – through a focus on containing warfare and state violence, the question of capitalism is made political, after all. This was the argument of the base as pressure point in *Afflicted Powers*.

The problem is well indicated by what these lines imply. The root must be challenged through the system's pressure points. Anything less will be futile. And yet such opposition risks, and needs to avoid, escalations to total war: where none can win, all will lose.

In the need for strategic indirection, the Left can find common ground: the aim must be systemic, the root must be challenged, the pressure points pressed – but not too directly, not in desperate detonations or head-on attacks, and not by the rules of spectacle. Is this what Clark meant, after all? No, to terror? Possibly.

I believe these tensions can be lived with: metabolic realism all down the line, clarity about the aims of "disarm, power down and abolish," visions for a post-capitalist "world in which many worlds fit." But also: struggle forms and tactics prepared to stop short of existential escalations. Alert to the dangers, restrained and strong against impatience and provocations. Standing Rock and the ZAD are exemplary here. "Diversity of tactics" cannot in fact mean anything goes. It is better, and will indeed be safer, to lampoon the billionaires than to personally fill them with terror and dread.

Direct action, yes, but carefully, avoiding spectacular forms that will give the state its excuse, its ticket to ride. Realism and indirection, not pacifism or quietism. And certainly not accelerationism. Life after the Holocene will be hard – the force-field, even harder. So let the Left recover, regather, recompose, reskill, rethink. Meanwhile, a local practice of more-than-human commoning would be minor progress, a sane and generous way ahead, into the troubles. First steps, reparative steps, small ones and slow. But steps on firm ground.

Protests after Hegemony

Mikkel Bolt Rasmussen

The last decade and a half have been a time of unrest. As the French political anthropologist Alain Bertho has described in his book *Le temps des émeutes*, the early 2000s saw a sharp increase in the number of protests.1 Strikes and demonstrations took place throughout the 1980s, 1990s and 2010s, of course, and food riots were not uncommon in the Global South. However, after 2008, there was both a quantitative and qualitative shift, with far more widespread protests, demonstrations, occupations, riots and uprisings taking place in far more places around the world. As Dilip Gaonkar writes, these protests and riots are moving north, and are now also occurring in liberal democracies.[2]

In retrospect, we can point to the Arab revolts, the so-called Arab Spring – which broke out in December 2010 in Tunisia and quickly spread to Egypt and a number of countries in North Africa and the Middle East in the early months of 2011 – as the decisive turning point. These events marked the transition from a period characterised by an almost total absence of radical dissent to a situation, in which the ruling order

---

1   Alain Bertho, *Le temps des émeutes* (Paris: Bayard, 2009).

2   Dilip Gaonkar, "Demos Noir: Riot after Riot," Natasha Ginwala, Gal Kirn and Niloufar Tajeri (eds.), *Nights of the Dispossessed: Riots Unbound* (New York: Columbia University Press, 2021), 31.

was challenged.[3] In particular, the images from Cairo, where thousands of people took to the streets, occupying Tahrir Square and demanding Mubarak's removal, punched a hole in the "capitalist realism" and "just move along" discourse of late capitalist globalisation.[4] From Cairo, the protests spread to southern Europe, with demonstrators occupying squares in Athens, Madrid, and Barcelona, demanding an end to the austerity imposed by national governments at the behest of the European Commission, the IMF and the European Central Bank. Such policies were enacted in the wake of the financial crisis, which quickly turned into an economic and social crisis in many southern European countries. In summer 2011, London was the scene of violent riots, followed that autumn by Occupy Wall Street's occupation of Zuccotti Park in Manhattan. As the first wave of protests died out or was crushed, others erupted elsewhere.

The years since 2011 have been characterised by a discontinuous global protest movement that has moved back and forth across the world in a staccato pattern of shifts and leaps. The protests have been so widespread that both 2011 and 2019 were each proclaimed to be "a new May '68," and *Time* magazine chose the protester as its "Person of the Year" in 2011.[5] Some of the most prominent episodes of this new cycle include the Chilean student protests of 2011–2012; the Brazilian transport resistance of 2013; the Ukrainian Maidan move-

---

3   Cf. Beverly J. Silver and Corey R. Payne, "Crises of World Hegemony and the Speeding Up of History," Piotr Dutkiewicz, Tom Casier and Jan Scholte (eds.), *Hegemony and World Order* (London: Routledge, 2020), 17-31.

4   Mark Fisher, *Capitalist Realism: Is There no Alternative?* (Winchester: Zero, 2010).

5   Cf. Robin Wright, "The Story of 2019: Protests in Every Corner of the Globe," *The New Yorker*, 30 December 2019, https://www.newyorker.com/news/our-columnists/the-story-of-2019-protests-in-every-corner-of-the-globe

ment; Nuit debout and the Gilets Jaunes in France; the democracy movement in Hong Kong; the Sudan Commune; the Lebanese uprising; protests against racist police in the US, from Ferguson in 2014 to Minneapolis in 2020; the Iranian "Women, Life, Freedom" revolt of 2022; and the protests against Macron's pension reform in France in April 2023. Even the coronavirus pandemic and local lockdowns did not end the new cycle of protests and the "underground Bildung" that has been emerging for more than a decade now.[6] This was made abundantly clear by the response to the murder of George Floyd, which saw the most widespread protests and riots in the US since the late 1960s. A police station was burned down, and wealthy neighborhoods, not usually sites of protest, saw looting and fighting between police and protesters.

During 2021–2022, we briefly seemed to be in an intermezzo marked by post-pandemic exhaustion and the re-emergence of inter-imperialist strife, which threatened to bury simmering discontent and desperation in a new-old Cold War binaries that made acts of dissent difficult. But it was only a matter of time before people were on the streets again. Sri Lanka was followed by Iran, and France is once again the scene of mass protests. Wherever we look, we see the socio-economic

---

6   The Danish Bordigist Carsten Juhl uses the description "underground *Bildung*" to describe the new protests and the latent revolutionary perspective observable within them. Carsten Juhl, *Opstandens underlag* (Copenhagen: OVO Press, 2021), 35.

conditions for more unrest.[7] Manufactured culture wars, often presented as intergenerational conflicts, are only the tip of the iceberg. Beneath the surface lies a crisis-ridden capitalism that seems unable to act strategically in the face of an accelerating climate crisis and stalling growth, which just never really seemed to gain any momentum after 2008. Representatives of the global bourgeoisie, like Deutsche Bank's research team, have seen the writing on the wall and, like Bertho, now speak of "an age of disorder."[8] However, despite realising there is a crisis, it seems extremely difficult for the bourgeoise to develop any real plans for a major transformation of the economy. As the neo-Leninist collective of Alex Hochuli, George Hoare, and Philip Cunliffe write in *The End of the End of History*, the ruling classes seem unable to unite around a plan. Today, the Situationist Gianfranco Sanguinetti would not be able to write a report, under the guise of "the Censor," on how the ruling class will save the capitalist status quo through staged terrorist attacks and false flag operations.[9] Hochuli, Hoare, and Cunliffe describe the current situation as the "nervous breakdown of

---

7   There is evidently no direct casual relation between economic crises and mass protests that turn into revolts or revolutions. In the inter-war period, a whole generation of Marxists had to come to terms with the fact that "politics" does not necessarily swing to the left when the "economy" does so. Protests cannot be reduced to "economic" or "sociological" facts that can then be understood as somehow indicating causality. Indeed, it is difficult to identify the "origin" of a protest. As Walter Benjamin explained in "On the Concept of History," insurrections short-circuit both past and present, and suspend historical continuity. Following Benjamin, Adrian Wohlleben describes this process as one in which "potentially-political" or "ante-political" life forms are mobilised and put to use in protests. Adrian Wohlleben, "Memes without End," *Ill Will*, 17 May, 2021, www.illwill.com/memes-without-end

8   Deutsche Bank, "An Age of Disorder," 2020, *Deutsche Bank*, https://www. db.com/newsroom_news/2020/the-age-of-disorder-the-new-era-for-economics-politics-and-our-way-of-life-en-11670.htm

9   Censor, *Truthful Report on the Last Chances to Save Capitalism in Italy* [1975], *notbored*, https://www.notbored.org/censor.html

neoliberalism," in which Big Tech billionaires dream of travelling into space, while large parts of the political establishment would like nothing more than to hold out "four more years," or at most another decade or two (Biden instead of Trump, etc.).[10] It is not even possible to unite around "green capitalism." But the genie is out of the bottle. The economic crisis is now taking the form of inflation, and none of the normal solutions, such as raising or lowering taxes or stimulating or curbing consumption, seem to work. Rather, there seems to be an unarticulated consensus that a great deal of existing capital must be destroyed. Moreover, the longer the crisis lasts, the greater the level of investment in military and counter-insurgency equipment.[11] The COVID lockdowns provided governments around the world with even more tools to monitor and combat discontent, so there is every indication that conflict will become even more confrontational – such is the prediction of *Manifeste conspirationniste*.[12] People are increasingly prepared to resort to violence, not least in America. To put it bluntly, every housewife in Florida now seems to be an Oath Keeper, and many businessmen are Proud Boys. Trump was a prelude, a figurehead. Now the real forces are taking shape.

Many commentators have noted that protests over the last 10–12 years have been characterised by a striking absence of concrete demands and have rarely involved the drawing up of actual political programs. The Left Communist Jacques Wajnsztejn, of *Temps critiques,* disparagingly calls the

---

10   George Hoare, Philip Cunliffe and Alex Hochuli, *The End of the End of History: Politics in the Twenty-First Century* (Winchester & Washington: Zero, 2021), 73-76.

11   SIPRI (Stockholm International Peace Research Institute), "Trends in World Military Expenditure, *SIPRI Fact Sheet,* April 2021," 2022, www.sipri.org/sites/default/files/2022-04/fs_2204_milex_2021_0.pdf

12   *Manifeste conspirationniste* (Paris: Seuil, 2022), 371.

phenomenon "insurrectionism." Following the 2011 London riots, the Leninist neo-Marxist Slavoj Žižek wrote that the events were "a blind acting out," an expression of a more generalised deficiency. [13] As Žižek put it: "opposition to the system cannot be formulated in terms of a realistic alternative, or at least a coherent utopian project, but can only take place as a meaningless outburst."[14] Even when the opposition is expressed by a pessimistic, postmodern slogan of defeat – "it is easier to imagine the end of the world than an alternative to capitalism," as Fredric Jameson put it in his analysis of the major structural transformations he had previously labelled postmodernism – or even when Nuit debout, in the Place de la République in Paris in spring 2016, rejected this nihilistic messaging, they did so in a kind of abbreviated form: "Another end of the world is possible" ("Une autre fin du monde est possible"), yet without any corresponding utopian or political vision.[15] This is not the "another world is possible" of the alter-globalisation movement, which was in itself a far cry from the many socialist mottos of the twentieth century, but instead we simply get "another *end* of the world is possible." While Nuit debout rejected postmodern defeatism, this was not in the service of a vision of another world. There does not seem to be anything behind capitalism and its crisis, nor anything approaching on the horizon, either. Rather, what has prevailed is a resigned, slightly sarcastic critique. Capitalism was, and is, undoubtedly digging its own grave, but also ours. The ongoing climate crisis is only the most obvious expression of that

---

13 Jacques Wajnsztejn and C. Gzavier, *La tentation insurrectioniste* (Paris: Acratie, 2012), 7. Disparagingly, because within Left Communism, describing something an 'ism is the same as describing it as a style or ideology.

14 Slavoj Žižek, *The Year of Dreaming Dangerously* (London: Verso, 2012), 54.

15 Fredric Jameson, *The Seeds of Time* (New York: Columbia University Press, 1994), xii.

process – but, if nothing else, we can fight *against* capitalism's preferred method of ending the world. According to the occupiers of the Place de la République, *dissent is still possible.*

Nuit debout's slogan is highly revealing. While the new protests take many different forms, what they have in common is less a shared a vision of a different society and more their refusal itself. Of course, alternative forms of society are discussed in some movements, such as the American and French ones, but these never arrive at anything that can be said to constitute a genuine program. The protesters simply refuse to accept the situation.

We need to analyse this refusal. Waves of uprisings crash invariably into brick walls, and yet our language for understanding them does not help us break through them. We are confronted with a linguistic obstacle. In what follows, I will present a theoretical and historical trajectory in which revolutionary vocabulary inherited from prior generations gradually recedes and disappears. This trajectory tells the story of the "victory" of the workers' movement, followed by the disappearance of "the worker" and a long economic crisis. I will end by introducing the notion of refusal as presented by Maurice Blanchot and Dionys Mascolo in 1958 when confronted with de Gaulle's state coup in the midst of the Algerian war. Perhaps revisiting the notion of refusal will enable us to step closer to our current situation and identify a new approach to the difficulties we experience today.

Yellow Vests

There is no doubt that the mass protests, demonstrations and uprisings of the last decade have differed from each other. Donatella Di Cesare is right to ask whether we can use one single term for these divergent struggles.[16] Hardt and Negri noted in 2013 that "each of these struggles is singular and oriented toward specific local conditions" but also went on to argue that the protests did indeed constitute a "new cycle of struggles."[17] Di Cesare agrees. Many of the protests acknowledged each other across borders and contexts, with Occupy activists mentioning the Tahrir protesters in Cairo and Egyptian revolutionaries ordering pizzas for the park occupiers in Manhattan. Syrian revolutionaries supported the Yellow Vest movement and proclaimed that "our struggle is common. [...] You cannot be in favour of a revolution in Syria while siding with Macron."[18] Not only did the protesters refer to each other, but the protests also shared tactics – the occupation approach utilised in Egypt, which saw the occupation of squares and roundabouts, spread first to Spain and the United States, and then to Turkey, Ukraine and France, among other places. Later in 2019, the frontliner tactics from Hong Kong began to spread elsewhere.[19]

One of the most striking features of the new cycle of protests has been the loose organisation and absence of demands. Of course, as Hardt and Negri pointed out, virtually all uprisings, demonstrations and occupations are directed against specific local or national conditions, but in the vast majority of cases, recent protests have not been accompanied by overarching political demands. In some protests, this lack of a program

---

16   Donatella Di Cesare, *The Time of Revolt* [2020] (Cambridge: Polity, 2022), 8.

17   Michael Hardt and Antonio Negri, *Declaration* (New York: Argo Navis, 2013), 4.

18   Des révolutionnaires syriens et syriennes en exil, "Les peuples veulent la chute des régimes," *lundimatin*, 14 December, 2018, https://lundi.am/les-peuples-veulent-la-chute-des-regimes

19   For a useful analysis of the spread of tactics, see S. Prasad: "Blood, Flowers and Pool Parties," *Ill Will*, 2 January 2023, https://illwill.com/blood-flowers-and-pool-parties

formed part of a more elaborate tactic, encompassing various inclusive intersectional meeting tactics. This was the case, for example, in the Occupy movement, which – as Rodrigo Nunes argues – had a distinctly "horizontal dimension." In other cases, this lack of any program has seemed more like an expression of desperation or outright aversion to politics.[20]

A good example is the Gilets Jaunes movement. The French roundabout occupations started in November 2018 as a protest against the Macron government's proposed fuel tax surcharge, which was to come into force in 2019. However, the protesters never presented anything that could be said to constitute a genuine political demand that the Macron government could possibly fulfil. In this sense, the protests were anti-political – understood not as a pejorative description but as a term for the rejection of mainstream politics. Dissatisfaction with the new tax immediately extended to frustration with growing economic inequality and the rural-urban divide. There were too many demands and no – or too many – leaders or spokespersons. The protests did not take the form that political protests usually take in France, nor were they mediated by the organisations that have traditionally assumed the role of representatives of social classes, political groups and professions. None of the major parties could claim with any great conviction that they were responsive to or could truthfully mediate the protests, although both Marine Le Pen and Jean-Luc Melenchon tried to position themselves as the legitimate political expression of the occupations – that is, until protesters looted shops on the Champs-Élysées and attacked the Arc de Triomphe. Quite simply, it was difficult to understand the protests within the framework of the existing political system and its vocabulary. Sociological studies showed that many

---

20   Rodrigo Nunes, *Neither Vertical nor Horizontal: A Theory of Political Organisation* (London & New York: Verso, 2021).

participants did not define themselves as significantly political, with roughly equal numbers voting for the Rassemblement National and what remains of the political Left in France. According to the sociologist Laurent Jeanpierre, the Yellow Vests broke the framework for understanding social movements in France by bypassing the institutions that have historically mediated and managed political protests.[21] The roundabout occupiers rejected not only the Macron government but also "the usual practices of social mobilisation." They shunned the workers' movement, occupied roundabouts in the countryside and semi-urban areas and did not shy away from confronting the police and looting shops. Politicians and media were quick to condemn the looting and "wild" demonstrations and could not figure out how to initiate dialogue with the diverse crowd of protesters. The protesters were so heterogeneous that it was not possible for Macron, his ministers, local politicians or the various parts of the French public sector to engage the Yellow Vests in political dialogue. Macron eventually withdrew the tax increase, yet people continued to take to the streets. In this way, the roundabout occupiers not only challenged the political order but constituted, in the words of Jeanpierre, an "anti-movement."[22]

In many ways, the Yellow Vests exemplify the new cycle of protest, much of which has taken place outside of traditional forms and channels of protest, alongside or in direct opposition to political parties and trade unions. It is more revolt than revolution, as Di Cesare writes,[23] more anarchism than

---

21   Laurent Jeanpierre, *In Girum. Les leçons politiques des ronds-points* (Paris: La Découverte, 2019), 19.

22   Ibid., 19.

23   Donatella Di Cesare, *The Time of Revolt*, 10.

communism, according to Saul Newman.[24] The demonstrators have been filled with anger, desperation, and hatred of the established political system. Marcello Tarì describes the many new protests as "destituent revolts," referring to Benjamin's notion of the *Entsetzung* of the general strike. As Tarì points out, protesters are not demanding anything from the political system, on the contrary, they are withdrawing their support, cancelling, as it were, their participation in political democracy, in whatever form this takes, from Tunisia to France to Chile.[25] As Tarì's friends from the Invisible Committee put it in their report on the first wave of protests up to 2014: "They want to oblige us to govern. We won't yield to that pressure."[26]

The key contours of this new cycle of protests can be discerned as early as the start of the 2000s before they really took hold at the turn of 2010–2011. In December 2001, hundreds of thousands of Argentines took to the streets to protest against the de la Rúa government's austerity plans, banging on pans and pots and shouting, "Que se vayan todos!" ("They all have to go!"). The Argentinian economy was in free fall after more than a decade of corrupt privatisation under the previous government's economy minister Domingo Cavallo, who enjoyed strong backing from the IMF and was therefore able to govern across party lines. De la Rúa had been elected in 1999 on a platform of change but soon reinstalled the ousted Cavallo, who continued to impose privatisation and austerity. Unemployment rose, and poverty exploded, but there was no change in policy. At the end of December 2001, the uprising broke out.

---

24 Saul Newman, *Postanarchism* (Cambridge: Polity, 2016), 49.

25 Marcello Tarì, *There is no Unhappy Revolution: The Communism of Destitution* [2017] (New York: Common Notions, 2021).

26 The Invisible Committee, *To Our Friends* [2014], https://ia601306.us.archive.org/17/items/01ToOurFriends/InvisibleCommittee-ToOurFriends-iweFinal-print.pdf

There were violent clashes, supermarkets were looted, and the police shot six demonstrators.

The Argentine activist collective Colectivo Situaciones, which itself took part in the fighting in Buenos Aires, subsequently described what happened in December as "a destituent uprising." Demonstrators did not take a stand in favor of opposition politicians or other parts of the Argentinean political system and refrained from demanding a softening of the IMF's austerity plan, the possibility of withdrawing money, or anything else specific. Instead, they demanded a break with the political-economic system in general. "If we talk about insurrection, then, we do not do so in the same way in which we have talked about other insurrections [...]. The movement of 19th and 20th [of December] was more a *destituent* [destituyente] action than a classical *instituent* movement," Colectivo Situaciones writes.[27] Those who took to the streets at the end of December in Buenos Aires and other cities across Argentina rejected the government and refused not only to give their support to other politicians but also to unite as a political subject, i.e. as people who assert their power to overthrow the existing order and institute a new one.

Central to Colectivo Situaciones' analysis was their identification of a shift away from the idea of establishing a counter or 'dual' power in the traditional Marxist sense. They argued that the demonstrators were not engaged in an attempt to overthrow the government or seize political power. They demanded not only the resignation of de la Rúa (which happened a few days later) but that all political representatives give up their mandates. The entire political system had to go. As Colectivo Situaciones describe it, a paradoxical political

---

27   Colectivo Situaciones, *19 or 20: Notes for a New Social Protagonism* [2002] (Wivenhoe & New York: Minor Compositions, 2011), 52.

subjectivation took place, in which the protesters did not become "the people" as a form of political sovereignty refusing to establish something new. "The revolt was violent. Not only did it topple a government and confront the repressive forces for hours. There was something more: It tore down the prevailing political representations without proposing others."[28] What was remarkable was the absence of a new constitution and the lack of any attempt to seize power.

If the seeds of the destituent insurgency model were sown in Argentina in 2001, it was in 2011 that they began to bloom. Colectivo Situaciones wrote insightfully about the complexities of describing the 2001 uprising, but the nature of it was ill-suited to the concepts Colectivo had adopted from Italian workerism and Latin American anti-imperialism. We see the same challenge echoed in the work of many commentators and analysts dealing with the new uprisings. A good example is the French philosopher Alain Badiou, who – in a series of books and articles from 2011 onwards – testifies to the great difficulty analysing the 2011 uprisings, the Arab revolts, the southern European square occupation movements, and the Yellow Vests.[29] According to Badiou, all of these movements lack an idea. They take to the streets to express discontent, but according to the veteran Maoist, they do not bring about change because they have no idea to which they are faithful. They are purely negative protests –and that's a problem. Badiou wants the protesters to develop a strategy, a new communist project akin to those of Lenin, Stalin and Mao in their

---

28   Ibid., 26.

29   Alain Badiou, *The Rebirth of History: Times of Riots and Uprisings* [2011] (London & New York: Verso, 2012); idem, *Greece and the Re-invention of Politics* [2016]; idem, "Lessons of the Yellow Vests Movement" [2021], *Verso blog*, https://www.versobooks.com/en-gb/blogs/news/4327-alain-badiou-lessons-of-the-yellow-vests-movement.

time. In doing so, he reveals his continued support for a state model of social happiness: the Yellow Vests and the other protest movements lack discipline and direction – in other words, organisation. Badiou rebukes those who take to the streets, beating them over the head with handed-down notions of revolutionary practice. In doing so, he paradoxically ends up imprisoning the protesters in a historical deficiency: they are not a revolutionary movement precisely because they do not have a particular (historically compromised) idea (of socialism and communism).

Badiou's pedantic analysis of the new cycle of protests is just one example of the difficulties many have when confronted with the new protests and their apparent lack of recognisable revolutionary or reformist slogans and political gestures. The late Zygmunt Bauman explained that protesters "are looking for new, more effective means of winning political influence, but [...] such methods have not been found yet."[30] With a mixture of condemnation and resignation, the English art historian and former Situationist T.J. Clark ironically criticised the young people who looted shops in London in 2011: they rejected commodity capitalism, yet simultaneously affirmed it by stealing sneakers and iPhones.[31] The conclusion seems to be that the protesters are trapped in a closed circuit of images and, as such, do not have access to a critical position from which to formulate a coherent critique of the current order. Badiou, Bauman, and Clark all have a point, but their critique of the new movements has a patronising air about it and tends to dismiss the protests with a hurried comparative analysis of

---

30   Zygmunt Bauman, "Far Away from Solid Modernity: Interview by Eliza Kania," *R/evolutions*, vol. 1, no. 1, 2013, 28.

31   T.J. Clark, "Capitalism Without Images," Kevin Coleman and Daniel James (eds.), *Capitalism and the Camera: Essays on Photography and Extraction* (London & New York: Verso, 2021), 125.

past revolutionary moments. Instead, we should perhaps, like Colectivo Situaciones, emphasise the element of experimentation and try to describe it. Doing so would enable us to anchor the new protests in a longer historical trajectory, in which an earlier vocabulary disappears as the economy changes – yet without blaming the new protests for not continuing or reactivating earlier forms of protest. The truth is that the political-economic conditions have changed, eroding the premises for the previous models that Badiou and Clark long for. What is interesting is how the new movements attempt to formulate a critique in a situation of radical crisis and collapse.

The long crisis and the disappearance of the worker

The erosion of the historical vocabulary of protest must be rooted in a longer historical trajectory. This is precisely what the old left intellectuals have failed to do. This is a trajectory in which the Western workers' movement in the post-World War II period tended to merge with political democracy. As another old communist thinker, the workerist Mario Tronti somewhat polemically put it, it was democracy, not capitalism, that killed the labour movement as a dissident alternative.[32] As we know from another Italian philosopher, the Stalinist Domenico Losurdo, the bourgeoisie fought fiercely to avoid a so-cio-material transformation, in which ownership of the means of production would become a political issue.[33] Representative democracy became a way of ensuring that this question was

32   Mario Tronti, "Towards a Critique of Political Democracy" [2007], *Cosmos and History*, vol. 5, no. 1, 2009, 74.

33   Domenico Losurdo, *Liberalism: A Counter-History* [2005] (London & New York: Verso, 2014).

never really formulated, or at least was formulated in a way that never called into question the capitalist mode of production's logic of accumulation.

During the interwar period, the vision of a different society beyond wage labour and the division of labour slowly but surely began to evaporate from European social democratic parties and disappeared for good in the post-war consumer society. Labour-market reforms by socialist parties – exemplified by Gerhard Schröder's Hartzen reforms in the 1990s – constituted the farcical phase of this development. If democracy was still a term for the rule of the poor in the 1840s, and Marx and Engels could therefore call themselves democrats, in the 20th century, the meaning of the term slowly transformed to mean majority rule and representation. This involved the implementation of various institutional processes aimed at ensuring that private property rights remained untouched so that the bourgeoisie not only maintained its economic power, but also extended it into the political dimension. As Lenin never tired of emphasising, the bourgeoisie has a head start in democracy because it owns "9/10 of the best meeting halls, and 9/10 of the stocks of newsprint, printing presses, etc."[34] Therefore, he continues, in a heated debate in 1918 with German Social Democrats like Kautsky and Schneidemann, elections never take place "democratically." The European Social Democrats did not follow Lenin's advice but began to participate in the national democratic competition. They did so initially because they believed that democracy was the most favorable terrain for the overthrow of capitalism. As is well known, this did not turn out to be the case. This is why Tronti passes such a harsh judgement on national democracy, describing it as the bane of the workers' movement. In retrospect, it is clear that

---

34   V.I. Lenin, "'Democracy' and Dictatorship" [1918], *marxists.org*, https://www.marxists.org/archive/lenin/works/1918/dec/23.htm

political democracy transformed the workers' movement from an external dissident force into an integral part of a political-economic system based on exploitation and accumulation. Admittedly, it was only after two world wars, a deep economic crisis and the emergence of fascism that political democracy managed to mediate the struggle between labour and capital, and the bourgeoisie began to feel confident about the working classes' allegiance to various national communities. The conflict within the class-divided society was resolved with political rights, cheap commodities, and welfare.

A more positive account of this historical trajectory is found in the work of Michael Denning, who argues that the labour movement pressured the bourgeoisie to extend the franchise and establish what he calls "the democratic state."[35] Denning reads the establishment of this state form as a victory, but at the same time acknowledges that victory was short-lived and, in retrospect – i.e. after neoliberal globalisation (Denning calls the period since the mid-1970s "the new enclosures" citing the Midnight Notes Collective) – appears hollow. The establishment of the welfare state, which Étienne Balibar calls "the social nation-state," was a victory for the workers' movement insofar as many more subjects (in the "First World," i.e. Western Europe and the United States) were not only recognised as political subjects (as citizens) but also, to a large extent, gained access to steady jobs, education, culture, and cheap, mass-produced goods.[36] The democratic nation-state emancipated urban working families from the poverty brought about by the agrarian revolution and industrialisation. However, at the

---

35   Michael Denning, "Neither Capitalist, Nor American: Democracy as Social Movement," *Culture in the Age of Three Worlds* (London & New York: Verso, 2004), 209-226.

36   Etienne Balibar, *We, the People of Europe? Reflections on Transnational Citizenship* [2001] (Princeton & Oxford: Princeton University Press, 2004), 61.

same time, it also led to the gradual neglect of the dream of a more radical supersession of capitalist society, its particular compulsions and its forms of alienation. Not only was the factory still hell for many women, young people, and migrants, but they were all still subject to patriarchal rule, both at home and at work. Add to this the neo-colonial restructuring of the world economy after 1945, and the post-war welfare state appears considerably less admirable. Welfare and nationalisation "at home" went hand in hand with neo-imperialism in the former colonies, exemplified by Clement Attlee's "progressive" Labour government, which in the late 1940s and early 1950s nationalised the health service, transport, and much of the industry in Britain, yet imposed sanctions on Iran when newly elected Prime Minister Mohammed Mosaddegh nationalised the country's oil industry. Later, in collaboration with the US, Attlee's government helped the Iranian military carry out a military coup to reinstate the Shah.[37]

The experimental 1960s were an attempt to reject gerontocratic power and challenge the rigid institutions of the welfare state in order to give everyday life an aesthetic boost. May '68 can be read as an attempt to reactualise the vision of a different life as a social revolution – partly as a rediscovery of the revolutionary proletarian offensive of 1917–1921. However, these experiments still took place within the framework of the ideas of socio-material transformation to which the workers' movement had formulated various responses throughout the 19th and 20th centuries with a view to replacing one (state)

---

37   Cf. Kojo Koram, *Uncommon Wealth: Britain and the Aftermath of Empire* (London: John Murray, 2022).

power with another.[38] The New Left was precisely that – a new Left – or as Stuart Hall put it, the New Left worked both with and against Marxism in an attempt to develop it.[39] For Hall and the New Left, Marxism (understood broadly as the workers' movement's reformist and revolutionary project of abolishing capitalism through a different kind of governance) was still the horizon. It was only with the movement of 1977 in Italy that a scathing critique of the Left truly emerged: "After Marx, April," as the Metropolitan Indians wrote on the walls of Bologna in February of that year.

Marxism is no longer our horizon. This is what we see in the new protests, which take place beyond the theory of class struggle, the dictatorship of the proletariat and the proletariat as the subject of history, and without the huge institutional infrastructure that the workers' movement built in the capitalist society. In a somewhat crude, materialist turn of phrase, industrialisation enabled the workers' movement to take up the struggle with the bourgeoisie, gain influence and participate in the management of national production. According to John Clegg and Aaron Benanav of *Endnotes*, "industrialisation was to be the driver of workers' incipient victory" since it brought growing numbers of industrial workers, growing unity among workers, and growing workers'

---

38   This was exemplary in the case of most Western Maoists of the period, who remained attached to a notion of power and a power alternative. The Situationists made progress in dissolving the idea of another form of power. They were critical of Socialists, Leninist and Maoists, but as was the case with the May '68 movement in general, they upheld an idea of another way of running production. In the case of the Situationists, this was to be done via councils.

39   Stuart Hall, "Cultural Studies and its Theoretical Legacies," Lawrence Grossberg, Cary Nelson and Paula Treichler (eds.), *Cultural Studies* (London & New York: Routledge, 1992), 279.

power in production."[40] However, now that industrialisation appears to be over, the workers' movement, in the various forms developed throughout the 20th century, is no longer able to organise opposition to exploitation and the dominance of capital. As the Italian Marxist Amadeo Bordiga and others have emphasised, capitalism is, first and foremost, a process of underdevelopment.[41] In the post-war period, the picture was different. Focusing on developments in the West, you could almost be forgiven for thinking that capitalism was engaged in making material deprivation part of history. However, since the early 1970s, global capital has been undergoing one extended crisis – what left communist Loren Goldner calls "the long neoliberal crash landing" – with falling productivity and growth rates that never reached the levels of the post-war boom.[42] This is the context of the disappearance of the workers' movement.

The French left-communist group Théorie communiste has described this transition as a departure from "programmatism."[43] From the mid-19th century until the end of the 20th century, revolution was a question of workers' power. It consisted of workers affirming themselves as workers, whether through the dictatorship of the proletariat, soviets or various forms of self-government. The revolution was a program to be realised, one

---

40 John Clegg and Aron Benanav, "Crisis and Immiseration: Critical Theory Today," in: Werner Bonefeld et al. (eds.), *The Sage Handbook of Frankfurt School Critical Theory* (London: Sage, 2018), 1636.

41 Amadeo Bordiga, *Strutture economica e sociale della Russia d'oggi* (Milan: Edizioni il programma comunista, 1976).

42 Loren Goldner, "The Historical Moment That Produced Us: Global Revolution or Recomposition of Capital," *Insurgent Notes*, no. 1, 2010, http://insurgent-notes.com/2010/06/historical_moment/

43 Théorie communiste, "Prolétariat et capital. Une trop brève idylle?," *Théorie communiste*, no. 19, 2004, 5-60.

that would end with the proletariat coming into its own and overcoming the contradictions of class society. The worker was the positive element in this contradiction, the one who would realise the future society. Programatism, be it socialist reformism, Leninism, syndicalism or council communism, was based on a link between the accumulation of capital and the reproduction of the working class. The development of capitalist modes of production only strengthened the workers (although they also became increasingly exploited by intensified labour processes). However, according to Théorie communiste, this link no longer exists. The worker has disappeared and no longer constitutes a point of departure for collective, organised resistance. During World War II and the post-war period, the large apparatus established by the workers' movement became part of the national social state and appeared less and less as an alternative to anything. Subsequently, as a result of the extensive reorganisation of the economy that began in the mid-1970s, the identity of the worker was emptied of content – a development often termed neoliberalism, globalisation or post-Fordism. In the old centres of capital the reorganisation took the form of de-industrialisation, outsourcing, precarisation, cuts in welfare programs, and a vast expansion of financial speculation, in which the production of value was detached from the direct production process.

In late capitalism, the worker is no longer an investment but merely an expense to be minimised. The Keynesian idea of a wage/productivity trade-off was replaced by the ever-increasing pursuit of lower costs. According to Théorie communiste, this shift constituted a counter-revolutionary response to proletarian resistance – and to May '68 in particular. As they put it: "There is no restructuring of the capitalist mode of production without a defeat for the worker. This defeat was a defeat for the identity of the worker, the communist parties, trade unions, self-management, self-organisation, and the rejection of work. It was a whole cycle of struggle that was defeated in all its aspects, the restructuring was essentially a counter-revolution."[44]

However, as economists and historians such as Ernst Mandel and Robert Brenner have shown, this restructuring did not have the desired effect, and the world economy has been shrinking since the mid-1970s.[45] The counter-revolutionary attack on the workers was insufficiently radical and therefore failed to establish a basis for a new class compromise. The bourgeoisie has destroyed more than it has built. This is the point of Goldner's characterisation of the last 40–50 years as one long unravelling or crisis, with rising unemployment, falling real wages, and cuts in social reproduction in the US and Western Europe. In many other parts of the world, the situation has been much worse. Local modernisation processes in China and South-East Asia cannot hide this – and even there, the number of poor workers and peasants has increased exponentially.

This is the political-economic background to the erosion of the anti-capitalist language that characterised the revolutionary projects of the second half of the 19th century and the "short" 20th century, the "century of extremes," as Eric Hobsbawm called the period from 1914 to 1989.[46] In Marx's terms, the working class and the proletariat begin to drift apart during the 1970s. Thus, when the new cycle of protest erupted in 2011, it did so in a historical void, "far from Reims" and

---

44   Ibid., 51.

45   Robert Brenner, *The Economics of Global Turbulence: The Advanced Capitalist Economies from Long Boom to Long Downturn, 1945–2005* (London & New York: Verso, 2006); Ernst Mandel, *Late Capitalism* [1972] (London: New Left Books, 1975).

46   Eric Hobsbawm, *The Age of Extremes: The Short Twentieth Century* (London: Michael Joseph, 1994).

displaced from the workers' movement, from its forms of resistance, and from the identity of the worker.[47] This is why most protests are not workplace protests but take the form of anti-political protests or looting. They are what Joshua Clover in a rather schematic historical analysis calls "circulation struggles," in which protesters take what they can from shops and the "market."[48]

Following Asef Bayat, who describes the Arab revolts as "revolutions without revolutionaries," *Endnotes* has suggested describing the new protest movements as "non-movements" that produce "revolutionaries without a revolution."[49] *Endnotes* also enthusiastically describes how many of the protests of the past decade have emerged out of nothing. A Chilean high school student posts a call for a demonstration on Facebook,

---

47   "Far from Reims" refers to Didier Eribon's book *Retour à Reims,* in which Eribon, now a Paris-based professor of philosophy, returns to Reims, where he grew up. He describes how his working-class family have become supporters of Front National (Rassemblement National). Eribon's story takes on the form of a melancholic analysis of this shift, in which workers who used to vote for the French Communist Party have ended up supporting Le Pen. However, this shift can also be seen as a form of continuity, because from 1944 onwards, the PCF did its best to support the notion of the nation – and in May '68 not only distanced itself from, but critiqued the revolt, and did its best to discredit it (including engaging in the antisemitic slandering of Daniel Cohn-Bendit).

48   Joshua Clover, *Riot. Strike. Riot: The New Era of Uprisings* (London & New York: Verso, 2016), 28.

49   Asef Bayat, *Revolution without Revolutionaries: Making Sense of the Arab Spring* (Stanford: Stanford University Press, 2017); Endnotes, "Onward Barbarians," *Endnotes,* 2021, https://endnotes.org.uk/other_texts/en/endnotes-onward-barbarians. Comparing the 2011 revolution to the Iranian Revolution, Bayat writes: "I find the speed, spread, and intensity of the recent revolutions extraordinarily unparalleled, while their lack of ideology, lax coordination, and absence of any galvanizing leadership and intellectual precepts have almost no precedent. [...] Indeed, it remains a question if what emerged during the Arab Spring were in fact revolutions in sense of their twentieth-century counterparts." Asef Bayat: *Revolution without Revolutionaries,* 2.

mobilising tens of thousands of protesters. A police killing rapidly exploded in the most violent protests in recent US history since the late 1960s. A French lorry driver, street racing in his tuned car, calls for a protest against the Macron government's new taxes and gathers more than 300,000 signatures in a matter of days. Each time, the protests seem to emerge far outside pre-existing parties and trade unions, which – at best – can only try to connect with these mobilisations or attempt to harness the energy they generate. However, even that is difficult. The fate of the various anti-political political parties, not least Podemos and Syriza, is testimony to this. As things stand, they are merely "weak social democracies."[50] Simply put, it is difficult to translate "non-movements" into state politics. The vast majority of participants do not belong to existing organisations but protest beyond the current political horizon. This is a "process" in the sense described by Verónica Gago in her analysis of the Ni Una Menos movement. It entails crossing a line from which there seems to be no possibility of returning to rejected political forms.[51]

Endnotes is, of course, affirmative with regard to the autonomy of protests. Following left communists such as Jacques Camatte, *Endnotes* writes that protests now seem to be characterised by an immanent dynamic by which they produce their own subjects. However, as the term "non-movement" indicates, this analysis is, as Kiersten Sol thar argued, characterised by a certain melancholy: protests take place, but they lack form, they do not constitute a movement.[52] The crisis of capital

---

50   Susan Watkins, "Oppositions," *New Left Review*, no. 98, 2016, 27.

51   Veronica Gago, *Feminist International* [2019] (London & New York: Verso, 2020), 12.

52   Kiersten Solt, "Seven Theses on Destitution," *Ill Will*, 2021, https://illwill.com/seven-theses-on-destitution.

pushes people onto the streets, but since there is no longer an organised workers' movement, nor any notion of workers as the proletariat, the protests are caught in an identity-political self-reflection, in which class struggle has become individual resistance, enacted together in the streets. The protests do not constitute a movement in the sense that both the established workers' movement and the "other workers' movement" did.[53] Rather, they are first and foremost characterised by disintegration and fragmentation. However, perhaps we should see the absence of the workers' movement as a precondition for the new protests rather than a shortcoming.

Judith Butler attempts to do this in her analysis of the squatting movements, in which she discusses precarity as the condition of possibility for a new subject of resistance: "Precarity is the rubric that brings together women, queers, transgender people, the poor, the differently abled, and the stateless, but also religious and racial minorities."[54] Butler shows how the subject of the new protests must necessarily struggle for a commonality that transcends the individual case. However, she does not really explain how the particular and the universal are linked – through acts of will or as a result of material processes? – and she, unfortunately, anchors her analysis within the framework of political representation and democracy. The point, however, is that there is no need to look back nostalgically, as *Endnotes* does in "Onward Barbarians" since the workers' movement has usually historically prevented the proletariat from becoming the class-destroying class. Communism is "a defeat from within" – this was the lesson Walter Benjamin drew from the

---

53   Cf. Karl Heinz Roth, *Die 'andere' Arbeiterbewegung und die Entwicklung der kapitalistischen Repression von 1880 bis zur Gegenwart: Ein Beitrag zum Neuverständnis der Klassengeschichte in Deutschland* (München: Trikont, 1974).

54   Judith Butler, *Notes Towards a Performative Theory of Assembly* (Cambridge, MA: Harvard University Press, 2015), 58.

Kapp-Lüttwitz Putsch and the slaughter of the Ruhr uprising in 1920.[55] Left communists like Camatte are no doubt very aware of that fact.

The aesthetics of rejection

If we are to supplement *Endnotes*' more sociological and melancholic description of the new protests with a less defeatist, political-aesthetic terminology, we can go back to the late 1950s, when Maurice Blanchot, along with Dionys Mascolo and others, tried to think through the possibility of another, new form of resistance, outside of the workers' movement, the state and politics in general. Throughout the history of the workers' movement and the revolutionary tradition, there have been plenty of attempts to bypass the movement's institutions, from wildcat strikes to DIY actions. However, this wild socialism – which in the case of Blanchot and Mascolo we might call literary communism – has usually been overshadowed by the established workers' movement. We see this in *Endnotes*, which melancholically analyses the shortcomings in the new protests against the background of the disappearance of the "worker."

In two short texts from May 1958, Blanchot and Mascolo develop a notion of radical refusal[56] in response to de Gaulle's

---

55   From "A Critique of Violence" in 1921 to "On the Concept of History" in 1940, Benjamin stressed that the workers' movement was opposed to the revolution, and that, as Bini Adamczak writes, communism constitutes a kind of "inner defeat." Cf. Bini Adamczak, *Yesterday's Tomorrow: On the Loneliness of Communist Specters and the Reconstruction of the Future* [2007] (Cambridge, MA: MIT Press, 2021).

56   For a presentation of the texts, see Mikkel Bolt Rasmussen, "An Affirmation That is Entirely Other," *South Atlantic Quarterly*, no. 1, 2023, 19-31.

coup d'état in early summer that year.[57] The old general had effectively used the Algerian liberation struggle, which appeared on the brink of spreading to France, to maneuver himself into position as president. The settlers and the French army in Algeria were in revolt and threatened to invade Paris if de Gaulle was not installed as head of government. The threat of an invasion prompted President René Coty not only to resign but also to plead with Parliament to allow de Gaulle to set up a temporary emergency government with extended powers.

The accelerated events of May–June 1958 led Blanchot and Mascolo to formulate a notion of radical refusal. Faced with this development, Mascolo – a former resistance fighter who had been expelled from the French Communist Party, an editor at Gallimard and a philosopher who wrote very little – in collaboration with the young surrealist Jean Schuster, launched the journal *Le 14 Juillet* to address the situation. In the first issue, Mascolo contributes a short text entitled "Unconditional Refusal," in which he writes: "I cannot, I will never accept this."[58] For Mascolo, the refusal was directly linked not only to the soldiers who deserted the French army but also to the Algerian revolutionaries who refused to speak under interrogation: "To speak like that in reality, to say no, and to justify this refusal, is to refuse to speak – I mean refuse to speak to the interrogator, and if it is authorised to make that claim, under torture."[59] Mascolo could not have more forcefully problematised the anti-fascist consensus on which the post-war political opinion rested – and of which the French Communist

---

57   For a detailed (albeit pro-de Gaulle) account of the events, see Odile Rudelle, *Mai 58. De Gaulle et la République* (Paris: Plon, 1988).

58   Dionys Mascolo, "Refus inconditionnel" [1958], *La révolution par l'amitié* (Paris: La fabrique, 2022), 28.

59   Ibid., 29.

Party was a part. France had to get out of Algeria. The Algerian revolutionaries had the right to rebel. Indeed, their struggle was not unlike the French resistance during World War II.

In his short text, Mascolo presented a perspective that made it important to speak out, effectively forcing the intellectual to take a stand, quickly and immediately, against society, in favour of another community founded on the rejection – or the impossibility – of accepting the events. "I cannot, I will never accept this. *Non possumus* ['We cannot,' Latin in the text]. This impossibility, or this powerlessness, that is our very power."[60] It was necessary to refuse the political "solution" – de Gaulle back in power – even without putting something else in its place.

In the following issue of the journal, Blanchot contributed a short text entitled "The Refusal." "At a certain moment, when faced with public events, we know that we must refuse. Refusal is absolute, categorical. It does not discuss or voice its reasons. This is how it remains silent and solitary, even when it affirms itself, as it should, in broad daylight."[61] Blanchot refused. He said no. A "firm, unwavering, strict" no. Blanchot not only rejected de Gaulle, but politics in general. It was what he later described as "a total critique," directed against the techno-political order of politics and the state.[62]

The rejection was absolute. It did not invite negotiation. It did not propose anything. For those who rejected, there was no compromise. De Gaulle was the compromise. The threat of military occupation of Paris was part of the compromise that

---

60   Ibid., 28.

61   Maurice Blanchot: "Refusal" [1958], *Political Writings, 1953-1993* (Fordham University Press, 2010), 7.

62   Maurice Blanchot: "[Blanchot to Jean-Paul Sartre]" [1960], ibid., 37.

allowed de Gaulle to appear as a solution as if he came to power naturally. He was just *there*. Once again, he was the saviour of France. In 1958 as in 1940. Blanchot rejected this entire process. The political game. Coty, Mitterrand, de Gaulle and the military. There was no need to explain his rejection. It was absolute.

Blanchot rejected de Gaulle and the false choice between civil war or the general – the civil war was already underway in Algeria and continued after de Gaulle came to power – but he also refused to formulate a political demand, a different path, a different solution. The refusal was "silent." In this way, there was a difference between Blanchot's refusal and other contemporary interventions (Roland Barthes, Socialisme ou Barbarie, the Situationists, etc.) that took the form of political analyses and mobilisation. Blanchot did not mobilise. The rejection was, of course, a political intervention – or, at least, an intervention in politics. Previously, Blanchot had explicitly refrained from engaging in political debate.[63] Now, he had returned to the fray. Or rather, he had not. The refusal was not an engagement with politics, but a cancellation of the political – and of the logic of representation that governs politics.[64]

---

63   As is well known, in the 1930s Blanchot was part of the French Far Right, writing a series of explicitly nationalist articles in different journals, including *Combat*. In 1940, he abandoned these links and refrained from participating in any kind of public political discussion. When he returned in 1958, it was, in the words of Philippe Lacoue-Labarthe, as "a kind of communist." Lacoue-Labarthe describes Blanchot's movement from French fascism to "a kind of communism" as a "conversion." Philippe Lacoue-Labarthe, *Agonie terminée, agonie interminable. Sur Maurice Blanchot* (Paris: Galilée, 2011), 16.

64   At this moment, Blanchot was also using the notion of refusal in his analyses of contemporary literature. In 1959, he published a text on Yves Bonnefoy, titled "The Great Refusal," in which he discussed how the poet broke with a Hegelian dialectics that makes subject and object identical, and argued that poetry is a "relation with the obscure and unknown." Maurice Blanchot, "The Great Refusal" [1959], *The Infinite Conversation* (Minneapolis: University of Minnesota Press, 1993), 47.

The refusal did not give rise to a political community in any traditional sense. There was no identity, no nation, no republic, not even a working class, nor a program around which the community could unite. The rejection was anonymous. It did not present a program that could be placed alongside existing ones. It did not enter into a political discussion. Rather, it withdrew. As Blanchot put it, "the refusal is accomplished neither by us or in our name, but from a very poor beginning that belongs first of all to those who cannot speak."[65] The refusal was, therefore, a mute statement. It pointed to a gap in representation and did not refer to any recognisable political subject.

In these two short texts, Blanchot and Mascolo outline a different kind of movement, a movement that rejects, that breaks with the state but also with the notion of politics as a new constitution, a revision of the law, a new law or a new government. It is a strange kind of revolutionary movement that does not recognise itself in a program or a party, that does not have a list of members, that emerges offering no promises, without the possibility of joining it. In the early 1980s, Blanchot, in dialogue with Jean-Luc Nancy, called it "the unavowable community," a community one cannot join or affirm as a political gesture. Refusal is an antagonistic gesture that abandons both *telos* and *arché*.

Of course, Blanchot and Mascolo's refusal draws on and is part of the Euro-modernist avant-garde, and its contribution to the notion of a communist revolution. Avant-garde movements, from Dada and Surrealism to the Situationist International, expanded historical materialism's notion of revolution, emphasising that the socio-material transformation must necessarily be accompanied by a psychological reorganisation. It was an understanding of the revolution as an open process, an

---

65   Maurice Blanchot, "Refusal," 7.

experiment in which there is no plan to be followed nor a program to be realised. The revolutionary process is both material and metaphysical. It concerns man, society and nature. In retrospect, we can say that the avant-garde and experimental art formed an important, often overlooked part of the revolutionary tradition.

As Debord explained in *The Society of the Spectacle*, Dada and Surrealism were not only contemporaneous with but part of the revolutionary proletarian offensive in the years after 1917. Among other things, their contribution was to make it clear that the revolution is not simply a question of who has power or how production is managed but concerns the whole of human life.[66] This is why the Surrealists sought to liberate the marvellous ("le merveilleux") and entered into an impossible collaboration with the French Communist Party: "Rimbaud and Marx" side by side, as Breton proclaimed.[67] Impossible, because the Russian Revolution quickly went off the rails: the Bolsheviks seized power and did everything to keep it, including crushing the anarchist Mahkno and the striking sailors in Kronstadt, militarising society, violently abolishing the peasantry, implementing an ecologically disastrous industrialisation, and destroying one revolutionary venture after another through the Comintern and the national communist parties – the French one being exemplary. The Surrealists realised that the revolutionary venture could only take place outside the Communist Party by means of what the Situationists later, following the end of modernism, called the "art of war." After World War II, COBRA, the Lettrist groups and the Situationists, continued the anti-artistic

---

66   Guy Debord, *The Society of the Spectacle* [1967] (New York: Zone Books, 1995), 136.

67   André Breton phrased it thus in the presentation he was not allowed to give at the International Congress of Writers in Defense of Culture.

and anti-political experiment, in which the "critique of everyday life" became an attempt to suppress art and politics as specialised activities in favour of satisfying humanity's radical needs.

With Blanchot and Mascolo, we are dealing with a different idea of revolution, in which the revolution does not end with the establishment of a new regime.[68] It is not about taking power but dissolving it. If it is a power, it is a power-dissolving power – "pouvoir sans pouvoir" ("power without power"), as Blanchot calls it.[69] It is an idea of a revolution that cannot be formulated as a new constitution, which cannot manifest in the form of rights. It is the movement as a post-metaphysical community, with no unity and no program, in which all of the political subjects (the citizen, the worker, the avant-garde, the multitude) disintegrate and where the revolution is an aim to be realised but a truth to be inhabited here and now. It is what Tarì and the Invisible Committee call "the destituent insurrection."[70]

My proposal is to complement the many good analyses of the new cycle of protests (Tarì, the Invisible Committee, Juhl, Di

---

68   Perry Anderson defines revolution as: "The political overthrow from below of one state order, and its replacement by another. [..] A revolution is an episode of convulsive political transformation, compressed in time and concentrated in target, that has a determinate beginning – when the old state apparatus is still intact – and a finite end, when that apparatus is decisively broken and a new one erected in its stead." It is precisely such an understanding of revolution Blanchot and Mascolo are trying to move beyond. Perry Anderson, "Modernity and Revolution," *New Left Review*, no. 144, 1984, 112.

69   Maurice Blanchot, "Literature and the Right to Death" [1949], *The Work of Fire* (Stanford: Stanford University Press, 1995), 331.

70   Marcello Tarì, *There is no Unhappy Revolution: The Communism of Destitution*; The Invisible Committee, *Now* [2017] (Los Angeles: Semiotext(e), 2017). See also the articles in the theme-issue of *South Atlantic Quarterly*, no. 1, 2023: "Destituent Power," edited by Kieran Aarons and Idris Robinson.

Cesare and Jeanpierre) with Blanchot and Mascolo's attempts to inspire a movement of refusal. Doing so makes it possible to analyse the new cycle of protests without having to refer to the disappearing workers' movement as a loss, as *Endnotes* tends to do. The new protests are occurring in the wake of programatism, but we do not need to hold up the different political forms and strategies of the workers' movement as a prism through which to interpret what has taken place since 2011. In fact, as Solt argues in her "Seven Theses on Destitution," this prevents an analysis of what is happening and reduces the revolution to a left-wing project.[71] Instead, a different insurrectionary movement is now underway. Instead of thinking of the new cycle of protests as a non-movement, we need to understand it as a radically open movement. It is what Giorgio Agamben, in a lecture on movements, referring to St Paul, has spoken of as a *hos me* movement, an "as not" movement – that is, a movement that does not assert an identity.[72]

An important point in Blanchot's and Mascolo's sketches is the autonomy that they argue characterises protests and revolts. As Carsten Juhl writes, when a protest becomes an uprising, it becomes its own substrate.[73] It is immanent, that is, it builds itself, but without the prospect of redemption. It creates what the Situationists called "positive voids," in which "everything that is done has a value in itself," as Furio Jesi writes in his

---

71   Kiersten Solt, "Seven Theses on Destitution."

72   The movement has to remain open, always coming. In his lecture on movements Agamben objects to a Schmittian understanding of movements as the political medium in which the people take on a political form. The task is to conceive of a movement that splits the people in two: *bios* and *zoe*. Agamben does not refer to Paul in his lecture, but Paul's understanding of the call is evidently the model for a different understanding of a movement that is not a movement.

73   Carsten Juhl, *Opstandens underlag*, 11.

analysis of the Berlin uprising of 1919.[74] *Endnotes* concurs in "Onward Barbarians," emphasizing that something new happens on the streets when people suddenly come together and challenge power. In other words, protests have an autonomy – an autonomy that we risk losing when we necessarily think of dissident protest in terms of a continuum of existing (or absent) political organisations.

The new protests take place in the dissolution of previous isms – socialism, communism, anarchism, Leninism, Maoism, etc. This is what Badiou finds so difficult to understand. Even *Endnotes* finds it difficult to affirm this disappearance. The new protests are anonymous, and the first thing that disappears is the self. In an atomised, late-capitalist world characterised by rapid identity fixes, individuality is, of course, immediately reintroduced. Late fascism is one desperate expressions of this, but so is the marketisation of protest, black bloc versus non-violent demonstrators, etc. We, therefore, start with this: the uprising is a rejection of society and commodity-based individuality. It is a dissolution of the self as individuality and as a political standpoint. As a signature. Even if people take to the streets in accordance with their identity (politics), a shift occurs when the uprising gets off the ground. It is not as an individual, class or mass that people take to the streets. Protests are radically unstable. They dispel the familiarity of late-capitalist life and dissolve all of the identities at our disposal. This is the "poor beginning" Blanchot described, the unarticulated refusal. In this sense, the movement that takes place is a disembarkation, the beginning of a more extensive escape. In it, no

---

74   Raoul Vaneigem and Attila Kotányi, "Basic Program of the Bureau of Unitary Urbanism" [1961], *cddc*, https://www.cddc.vt.edu/sionline/si/bureau.html; Furio Jesi, *Spartakus: The Symbology of Revolt* [1969/2000], (London & Calcutta: Seagull, 2014), 46.

one is interested in becoming "civil society's junior partner."[75] Rather, they are turning away from the community of capital, the money economy, the state, and the workers' movement – the last two being nothing more than "a fable for dupes."[76]

---

75   "Civil society's junior partner" is Frank B. Wilderson's term for movements that do not question anti-Black violence in the attempt to oppose present powers. Frank B. Wilderson III, "The Prison Slave as Hegemony's (Silent) Scandal," 2003," *Social Justice*, vol. 30, no. 2, 2003, 18-27.

76   The Invisible Committee, *Now*, p. 72.

Contributors

Mikkel Bolt Rasmussen is Professor in Political Aesthetics at the University of Copenhagen. He is the author of *Playmates and Playboys at a Higher Level: J.V. Martin and the Situationist International* (Sternberg Press, 2014), *Crisis to Insurrection* (Minor Compositions, 2015), *After the Great Refusal: Essays on Contemporary Art, Its Contradictions and Difficulties* (Zero, 2018), *Trump's Counter-Revolution* (Zero, 2018), *Hegel after Occupy* (Sternberg Press, 2018) and *Late Capitalist Fascism* (Polity, 2022), as well as a number of books in Danish, most recently *På råbeafstand af marxismen* (Antipyrine, 2019) and *Dialog med de døde* (Antipyrine, 2023).

Yves Citton is Professor in Literature and Media at the Université Paris 8 Vincennes-Saint Denis and co-editor of the journal *Multitudes*. He recently published *Altermodernités des Lumières* (Seuil, 2022), *Faire avec. Conflits, coalitions, contagions* (Les Liens qui Libèrent, 2021), *Générations collapsonautes* (Seuil, 2020, in collaboration with Jacopo Rasmi), *Mediarchy* (Polity Press, 2019), *Contre-courants politiques* (Fayard, 2018), *The Ecology of Attention* (Polity Press, 2016). Most of his articles are in open access online at www.yvescitton.net

Natasha Gasparian is a PhD candidate in Contemporary Art History and Theory at the Ruskin School of Art, University of Oxford. In addition to her art criticism, which has appeared in *Artforum, Camera Austria,* and *Texte Zur Kunst,* she is the author of *Commitment in the Artistic Practice of Aref*

El-Rayess: The Changing of Horses (Anthem Press, 2020). Gasparian is an organising member of the Beirut Institute for Critical Analysis and Research (BICAR).

Esther Leslie is Professor of Political Aesthetics at Birkbeck, University of London. Her books include various studies and translations of Walter Benjamin, as well as *Hollywood Flatlands: Animation, Critical Theory and the Avant Garde* (2002); *Synthetic Worlds: Nature, Art and the Chemical Industry* (2005); *Derelicts: Thought Worms from the Wreckage* (2014), *Liquid Crystals: The Science and Art of a Fluid Form* (2016) and *Deeper in the Pyramid* (2018) and *The Inextinguishable* (2021), both with Melanie Jackson.

Gene Ray is Associate Professor in the CCC Research Master Programme at Geneva University of Art and Design (HEAD-Genève, Hes-so). He is author of *Terror and The Sublime in Art and Critical Theory* (Palgrave Macmillan, 2005, 2011), editor of *Joseph Beuys: Mapping the Legacy* (D.A.P., 2001), and co-editor of *Art and Contemporary Critical Practice: Reinventing Institutional Critique* (Mayfly, 2009) and *Critique of Creativity: Precarity, Subjectivity and Resistance in the 'Creative Industries'* (Mayfly, 2011). His new book, *After the Holocene: Planetary Politics for Commoners*, is forthcoming with PM Press.

Abigail Susik is the author of *Surrealist Sabotage and the War on Work* (Manchester University Press, 2021), editor of *Resurgence! Jonathan Leake, Radical Surrealism, and the Resurgence Youth Movement, 1964-1967* (Eberhardt Press, 2023), and coeditor of the volumes *Surrealism and Film after 1945: Absolutely Modern Mysteries* (Manchester University Press, 2021) and *Radical Dreams: Surrealism, Counterculture, Resistance* (Penn State University Press, 2022). Susik is a founding board member of the International Society for the Study of Surrealism and an Associate Professor of Art History at Willamette University.

Marina Vishmidt is a writer and educator. She teaches at Goldsmiths, University of London. She is the co-author of *Reproducing Autonomy* (with Kerstin Stakemeier) (Mute, 2016), and the author of *Speculation as a Mode of Production: Forms of Value Subjectivity in Art and Capital* (Brill 2018 / Haymarket 2019). Her work has appeared in *South Atlantic Quarterly, Artforum, Afterall, Journal of Cultural Economy, e-flux journal, Australian Feminist Studies, Mousse,* and *Radical Philosophy,* among others, as well as a number of edited volumes. In 2022, she was the Rudolph Arnheim Visiting Professor in Art History at the Humboldt University in Berlin and will take up a professorship in art theory at the University of Applied Arts in Vienna in the autumn of 2023. Marina passed away in May 2024.

Milton Keynes UK
Ingram Content Group UK Ltd.
UKHW030608041024
449168UK00004B/110